CIRIA C669

D1382507

London, 2008

TELEPHONE 020 7549 3300   FAX 020 7253 0523
EMAIL enquiries@ciria.org   WEBSITE www.ciria.org

Half of all the people who die on a construction site have been working there for less than two weeks. Effective management action could have prevented **70 per cent of fatal** construction accidents.

A hazard is something with the potential to cause injury, eg an unsupported trench in clay soil.

Risk is the likelihood that the hazard will result in an accident. Risk also considers how serious the resultant injury would be and how many would be affected.

Site safety is not a nice to have option, it is a right for all engaged in construction. It is about education, empowerment and leadership, not process or policing. Without all involved sharing the belief we should and can have safe sites, hazardous behaviours will emerge that history tells us results in needless deaths and injuries.

This easy-to-use reference guide gives an overview to prepare you for working safely and it provides advice on what to do when you come across commonly encountered hazards or if an accident occurs.

The information will also assist designers to appreciate the site hazards which they need (under CDM2007) to identify, eliminate where possible and then reduce the level of residual risk.

Everyone on site should find it helpful and useful. It takes account of recent changes in health and safety legislation, for example the Work at Height Regulations 2005, and emphasises the need for all those involved in construction to identify, assess and manage risks, working together and co-operating as a team.

I am pleased that CIRIA has produced this revised handbook for the benefit of all those in the construction industry. I commend it to your use.

Keith Clarke
Chairman of the Health and Safety Committee
of the Construction Industry Council

Summary

Building and civil engineering construction sites contain many hazards. The risks to operatives, engineers, architects and surveyors – and especially to operatives and professionals going to work on them for the first time – are considerable.

This fourth edition of CIRIA's *Site safety handbook* has been prepared to alert operatives and construction professionals to the hazards often present on site, to provide advice on safer practices for themselves and others, and to help them manage these important responsibilities. It has been revised to reflect the recent changes in health and safety regulations.

Although the text is written in the context of the legal framework provided by the Health and Safety at Work etc Act 1974, the handbook is not a legal document nor is it a comprehensive manual on site safety. It is designed to be an easy-to-read, ready reference guide for use outside, which will slip easily into a pocket. To achieve its purpose, the text has been kept brief.

The text is divided into the following main parts:

- **Before going on-site** – four chapters explain the responsibilities of the professional and the preparations needed before going on-site
- **Site activities and safety hazards** – each of the chapters deals with a principal issue, eg falling from height
- **Your contribution** – three chapters explain what professionals should do to deal with hazards, assist with accidents and how to investigate them

References are listed at the end of each chapter.

The handbook starts with a foreword by Keith Clarke, chairman of the Health and Safety Commission.

> **For further information about health hazards on-site
> refer to CIRIA C670 *Site health handbook***

Site safety handbook (fourth edition)

Bielby, S and Gilbertson, A L

CIRIA

C669   © CIRIA 2008   ISBN 978-0-86017-669-5

First published 1992 (SP90), second edition 1997 (SP130), third edition 2001 (SP151)

British Library Cataloguing in Publication Data

A catalogue record is available for this book from the British Library

Keywords		
Health and safety, site management, regulation, construction management, project management, respect for people		
Reader interest	**Classification**	
Health and safety, site safety, site management, CDM2007	AVAILABILITY	Unrestricted
	CONTENT	Advice/guidance
	STATUS	Committee-guided
	USER	Construction professionals, architects, engineers, designers, surveyors, planners, site managers, site supervisors, site workers, construction managers, contractors, project managers/directors, local authority staff, CDM co-ordinators, regulators, construction clients

Published by CIRIA, Classic House, 174-180 Old Street, London EC1V 9BP, UK

Contents

Contents

Acknowledgements

This revision of CIRIA's *Site safety handbook* was carried out by Mr A L Gilbertson. Work has been funded by CIRIA who wishes to express its thanks to all who contributed to this and previous editions of the handbook:

CIRIA is grateful to the following who assisted with this work:

Ove Arup Partnership	Health and Safety Executive
WS Atkins Ltd	HMSO
Balfour Beatty Management	Institution of Civil Engineers
Building Employers Confederation	Royal Institution of Chartered Surveyors
Construction Industry Training Board	Thames Water Utilities
Costain Group	Travers Morgan Ltd
HMSO	RoSPA
V J Davies	CITB
Tiefbau Berufsgenosssenschaft	Habilis
Kier Group	WSP

CIRIA is particularly grateful to David Lambert of Kier Group, David Watson of WSP and Graham Leech of Balfour Beatty Management for assistance with the 2008 update.

Starting point

Construction professionals

Did you realise that every week (on average), someone dies on a British construction site? And that is something that legislation alone cannot change. This handbook is essential reading when you go on site, regardless of your job description. It is directly relevant to all construction professionals, including:

- civil engineers
- structural engineers
- architects
- quantity surveyors
- building services engineers
- project managers

- planners
- designers
- electrical engineers
- mechanical engineers
- building engineers
- surveyors
- facilities managers.

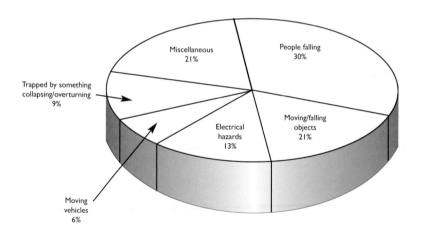

Miscellaneous
21%

People falling
30%

Trapped by something
collapsing/overturning
9%

Electrical
hazards
13%

Moving/falling
objects
21%

Moving
vehicles
6%

The major causes of construction deaths

 You have a 1 in 2 chance of injury during 20 years working on site.

Scope of the handbook

This handbook has been designed as a ready reference guide to advise construction professionals about health and safety and to help them to understand and manage health and safety in construction. *However, it is not a legal document nor is it a comprehensive manual.*

It highlights the common hazards that all people on site will be meeting from day to day. It promotes safer construction practices by explaining the basic safety standards to apply on construction sites.

> The handbook does not cover ionising radiation, compressed air, explosives, quarrying, diving, tunnelling, working in cofferdams, caissons or other specialist activities. Similarly, particular local hazards, such as working next to a live railway line, will require detailed analysis of the risks, including consultation with other parties. **All potential hazards must be identified and evaluated.** Specialist training is required for these activities.

The handbook is in three main sections:

1 Before going on-site.

2 Site activities and hazards.

3 Your contribution.

The section on *Site activities and hazards* consists of brief chapters arranged in alphabetical order. The figures illustrate basic safety points, but are not definitive working drawings.

It slips easily into your pocket so that it is at hand wherever and whenever you need it. This book could help save your life ... or the life of one of your colleagues.

This handbook has been written for you ... because safety on site is something you cannot afford to ignore, and **you** have statutory responsibilities for safety.

Starting point

You must work within this framework to manage health and safety:

Health and safety is integral to the responsibilities of everyone on site and must be exercised within a management framework. This includes:

- legal requirements
- your own company policy and its implementation
- specific site rules for safe systems of work
- professional codes of conduct and ethics.

As a professional, you can play an important part in helping to encourage safer construction practices and to prevent dangerous acts that could lead to accidents.

The law

If there is a conflict between health and safety legislation, contract requirements, company policy, site rules or professional ethics, then health and safety legislation takes precedence.

The Health and Safety at Work etc Act 1974 provides a comprehensive legislative framework for promoting, stimulating and encouraging high standards of health and safety in the workplace. The aim of the Act is to increase health and safety awareness and to promote effective standards in every organisation.

Everyone is involved: management, employees, self-employed, employees' representatives, those in charge of premises and the manufacturers of plant, equipment, substances and materials in matters of health and safety. The Act also deals with the protection of the public, where they may be affected by work activities.

The Act consists of four parts, but only Part one directly concerns you.

The main provisions of Part one of the Act seek:

- to ensure the health, safety and welfare of persons at work
- to protect persons other than persons at work against risks to health and safety arising out of, or in connection with, the activities of persons at work
- to control the keeping and use of explosive or highly flammable or otherwise dangerous substances
- to control the emission into the atmosphere of noxious or offensive substances
- to provide for criminal offences and punishments.

I Your responsibilities

The Act says that your responsibilities are:

a) To take reasonable care for the health and safety of yourself and others who may be affected by your acts or omissions at work.

b) To co-operate with your employer and any other person properly involved in all matters relating to health and safety law and any duty or requirement that the employer may be required to make under that law.

It is also an offence for any person intentionally or recklessly to interfere with or misuse anything provided in the interests of health, safety or welfare that the law may require.

You will also need to be familiar with the Construction (Design and Management) Regulations 2007 (CDM2007), which is now the central driving regulation for construction health and safety. CDM2007 places duties upon all parties affecting work on site, and as a professional you will have a personal duty requiring you to work with others in a spirit of co-operation and communication.

> If you are concerned by something you see or experience on site, under CDM2007 you must report it to your manager. As a professional you have a duty of care to inform whoever is in control of work on site of your concerns, as explained on page 17.

There are over 50 health and safety Regulations that may apply to work on construction sites. The Regulations which most affect the design and management of work are the Construction (Design and Management) Regulations 2007 (CDM2007) and the Management of Health and Safety at Work Regulations 1999 (the Management Regulations). These are regulations with which you need to be familiar, as they are the central driving regulations for preparing and planning for work.

CDM2007 places duties on the client and all parties who are resourcing, designing and preparing for works on-site. It requires all parties to co-operate with each other and those on adjoining sites, and to co-ordinate their activities to ensure works are carried out with health and safety an integral part of the management process.

The Management Regulations cover many health and safety matters. The most pertinent with regard to site safety and site health is that an employer must provide those working with details of the preventative and protective measures to carry out the activity safely (ie a safe method of working or method statement). They must also provide information of the risks to health and safety identified by a risk assessment to prepare that safe method of work (ie a suitable and sufficient risk assessment).

The premise on which this handbook is prepared is that any work activity must be carried out in accordance with a safe method of work. This safe method of work is derived from an assessment of the risks to the worker and those affected by the work matched with suitable preventative and protective (control) measures. A risk assessment is of no use unless a safe and healthy method of work is prepared using the results of that assessment.

Some Regulations cover hazards where the risks are considered so serious that safe methods of work are essential and specific risk assessments are required. These Regulations include:

- Provision and Use of Work Equipment Regulations 1998
- Manual Handling Operations Regulations 1992 (amended 2002)
- Personal Protective Equipment at Work Regulations 1992 (and Personal Protective Equipment Regulations 2002)
- Control of Asbestos Regulations 2006
- Control of Lead at Work Regulations 2002
- Control of Noise at Work Regulations 2005
- Control of Substances Hazardous to Health Regulations 2002 (COSHH)
- Control of Substances Hazardous to Health (amendment) Regulations 2004.

Both the Management and CDM2007 Regulations require that you report anything considered to be a health and safety issue to managers or supervisors.

Both sets of regulations also require and encourage you and others to work together in a spirit of co-operation and communication so that health and safety matters can be co-ordinated, not just within your organisation and your site, but with others on-site and on adjoining sites.

> **If you are concerned by something you are designing or managing or planning to do, or by anything you see or experience on site, you must report it to your manager or supervisor. As a professional, you also have a duty of care to inform whoever is in control of work on-site.**

I Your responsibilities

Company policy and its implementation

Every employer with five or more employees must provide a written statement of the company's general policy, organisation and arrangements for health and safety at work. The employers must show, or give this, to all employees and to keep it up-to-date.

A company's safety policy and arrangements will explain:

- what your employer intends should happen
- how the employer is going to set up and maintain a safe and healthy working environment
- what health and safety responsibilities exist
- who is responsible and how to contact them
- that safe systems of work exist and who is responsible for them
- the arrangements for review and update etc.

You must read this policy, understand your responsibilities and carry them out.

It is important that you know the organisational structure and whom you should ask for health and safety advice. Normally this will be your manager or the appointed safety adviser/supervisor for your site.

Risk assessment and management

The **Management of Health and Safety at Work Regulations** require that the risks associated with any hazardous work activity are assessed before work starts so that the necessary preventative and protective measures can be identified and put into place. This process of risk assessment starts at the planning stage of a project and continues during the construction phase. Risk assessment forms the basis of all recent health and safety legislation, and is the starting point for all construction management and safe systems of work.

CDM2007 places a duty to carry out a process of design risk management specifically upon designers. So far as reasonably practicable, hazards must be eliminated and risks reduced. In addition, information must be passed on to other people, to help them manage residual risk.

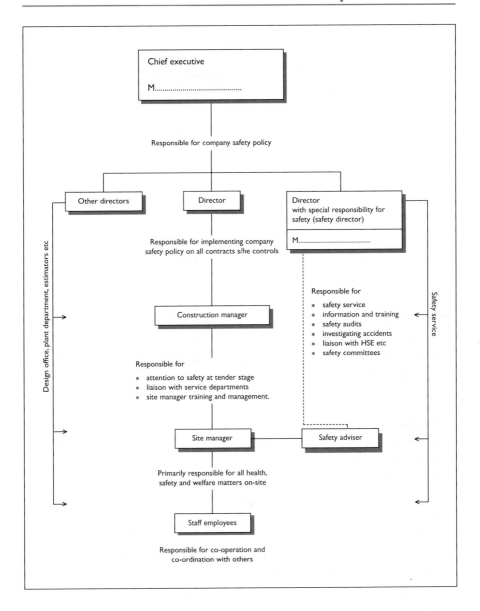

Responsibilities for health and safety in a typical company

1 Your responsibilities

Method statements for safe systems of work

Every site is unique and requires site-specific methods for safe systems of working for all hazardous operations. These are normally contained in written method statements prepared after hazards have been identified and risks assessed.

Note: following a risk assessment prepared for a hazardous activity, a method statement should be prepared.

The order of preparation should be:

1 Identify hazards.

2 Assess risks (identify who is at risk).

3 Reduce risks to acceptable level using the principles of prevention and protection (see page 22).

4 Specify control measures both preventative and protective

5 Prepare method statement.

A method statement will typically include information on:

- the person in charge of operations
- safe means of access to and from all work areas
- specific details of any lifting appliances, including positioning on site and lifting gear to be used
- details of storage of materials and methods for dealing with hazardous substances
- how the work is to be carried out
- communications
- the equipment to be used and protective clothing and equipment to be worn
- emergency arrangements (where required).

No deviation from the method statement should be allowed without referring back to the contractor who prepared it and a revised statement being produced. CDM requires the principal contractor to liaise with contractors before a construction phase plan is prepared.

Always ask to see the risk assessment for any potentially hazardous activity before you start work on that activity.

Professional codes of conduct

All members of professional bodies are bound by their code of conduct. For example, item 1 of the Rules for Professional Conduct of the ICE states that:

"A member, in his responsibility to his employer and to the profession, shall have full regard to the public interest, particularly in matters of health and safety."

Other institutions have similar rules.

Your actions

If you see a situation that, in your opinion, involves a risk of death or serious injury, you have a **statutory duty** to take immediate action.

This includes one or more of the following actions:

- tell the person in danger to stop, explaining why – but don't put yourself at risk in doing so
- contact the person in charge of the activity and your immediate manager and inform them of your actions
- later inform appropriate senior site personnel
- if you are uncertain about the degree of risk involved, consult the senior site manager before taking any further action and record it in your site diary.

If you ignore a danger you condone it and will share responsibility for any accident. Do not be put off or let yourself be overridden if you believe the danger exists. Things that look unsafe usually are.

Other risks should be dealt with through your formal channels of communication – refer the matter to your manager and your safety adviser. The HSE provides advice and guidance on health and safety matters. Consult it if you cannot get advice within your own organisation.

REMEMBER
Firms *and* individuals can be prosecuted. If in doubt, ask your immediate manager without delay. Never be frightened to ask to see a risk assessment if you believe the activity to be hazardous.

1 Your responsibilities – Bibliography

- HMSO (1974) *The Health and Safety at Work etc Act 1974* (ISBN 0-10543-774-3)

- HSE (1999) *Management of health and safety at work. Management of health and Safety at Work Regulations 1999. Approved Code of Practice,* HSE Books, London (ISBN 0-71762-488-9)

- Davies, V J and Tomasin, K (1996) *Construction safety handbook,* 2nd edn, Thomas Telford, London (ISBN 978-0-72772-519-6).

The Construction (Design and Management) Regulations 2007 (CDM2007)

When does CDM2007 apply?

CDM2007 applies to all construction projects. For notifiable projects, ie more than 30 working days or more than 500 person days of work, a CDM co-ordinator and a principal contractor are appointed by the client.

CDM may not apply in full to work for certain clients, eg domestic clients, but always applies to designers and contractors irrespective of the size and duration of the work. Further guidance on the application of CDM is given in the Approved Code of Practice (ACoP), *Managing Health and Safety in Construction.*

The term construction work has been widely defined in the CDM Regulations and includes virtually all activities within the building, civil engineering or engineering construction sectors of the construction industry.

Duties

The CDM Regulations place duties and responsibilities on clients, designers, CDM co-ordinators, principal contractors and contractors, to plan, co-ordinate and manage health and safety throughout all stages of a construction project. Co-operation also extends to those on adjoining sites.

A construction phase plan has to be prepared and developed by the principal contractor before work can start on site, and the client has to ensure that this plan complies with CDM2007. The principal contractor has to consult with contractors before work starts and review, revise and update the plan throughout the construction phase.

REMEMBER Consult the construction phase plan, as this details the management arrangements put in place for health and safety.

2 Construction-related regulations

Main duties of the five key parties

- **The client** – has to set up the project properly, engaging competent designers and contractors, and also appointing a competent CDM co-ordinator (CDM-C) and principal contractor for a notifiable project. The most demanding duty is to ensure that there are health and safety arrangements in place by the client and all others to ensure the health and safety of workers and others during the construction phase and in the future.

- **Designers** – have to design structures to avoid foreseeable risks to health and safety during construction, maintenance and cleaning work. Residual risks must be reduced so far as is reasonably practicable and information provided where necessary on the residual risks, not just for the initial construction phase, but also for the future work on the structures through information for the health and safety file. Design includes the preparation of specifications and the choice of materials and products – it is not limited to calculations and drawings. They also have to take account of the workplace hazards and of the Workplace (Health Safety and Welfare) Regulations if the structure will be used as a workplace.

- **The CDM co-ordinator (CDM-C)** – the organisation or person with responsibility for ensuring arrangements are made and implemented by the project team for co-operation and co-ordination of the health and safety aspects of the design work, the acquisition and provision of information relevant to health and safety issues, and the preparation of the health and safety file for each structure. The CDM-C may be principally involved with advising and assisting the client, especially in regard to the arrangements that need to be in place during design and construction.

- **The principal contractor** – has to prepare and continually review the construction phase plan and manages and co-ordinates the activities of all contractors. The duties also relate to the provision of information and training on health and safety for everyone on-site and the co-ordination of the views of the workers on-site. They also supply information for the health and safety files to the CDM-C as well as gathering information for the files from contractors.

- **Contractors and self-employed workers** – must co-operate with the principal contractor and other contractors and provide relevant information on the risks created by their work and how they will be controlled. They also contribute relevant information for the health and safety file.

Everyone must co-operate with others on their site and on adjoining sites, and should co-ordinate their work with others.

Construction-related regulations 2

Anyone arranging for others to do work should make sure those they engage or appoint are competent and sufficiently resourced to discharge their health and safety duties on that project. Full details are given in the ACoP.

Key requirements of CDM2007

CDM2007 includes specific key requirements for construction work including:

- proper planning and management of work on site
- provision of good quality welfare facilities for workers
- provision of information and training to workers
- consultation with workers
- safe places of work
- good order and site security
- stability of structures
- demolition and dismantling
- explosives
- excavations
- cofferdams and caissons
- reports of inspections
- energy distribution installations
- prevention of drowning
- traffic routes
- vehicles
- prevention of risk from fire etc
- emergency procedures
- emergency routes and exits
- fire detection and fire-fighting
- fresh air
- temperature and weather protection
- lighting.

The requirements of these Regulations have been reflected in this handbook.

Note that the content of the previous Construction (Health Safety and Welfare) Regulations (now withdrawn) is included in CDM2007, outlined above.

2 Construction-related regulations

The Management of Health and Safety at Work Regulations

These Regulations apply to all work, including construction. They include the requirement for employers (and the self-employed) to assess the risks arising from work activities.

The five steps to risk assessments

Step 1:   Look for the hazards

Step 2:   Decide who might be harmed and how

Step 3:   Evaluate the risks and decide whether the existing precautions are adequate or whether more should be done

Step 4:   Record your findings

Step 5:   Review your assessment and revise it if necessary

In selecting control methods, the principles and hierarchy of **prevention and protection** should be used:

- avoid risks altogether if possible
- evaluate remaining risks and reducing the level of risk
- combat risk at source
- wherever possible adapt work to the individual
- take advantage of technological progress
- ensure risk controls are part of a coherent policy
- protect the whole workforce rather than individuals (collective protection)
- ensure the control measures are understood by giving instructions and training.

Workers must be consulted and must be adequately trained to understand and implement the control measures. Employers must monitor the workplace to ensure that the control measures are implemented and effective; this will include appropriate health surveillance, eg lung function tests for spray painters.

> **REMEMBER**
> The use of **Personal Protective Equipment (PPE) should be the last – not the first – choice of risk control because PPE is the least effective means of risk management.**

- APS (2007) *Design risk management – advice for designers on the implications of the construction (Design and Management) Regulations 2007*, Riba Publishing, London (ISBN 978-1-85946-275-1)

- APS (2007) *Guide to the management of CDM co-ordination*, Code, 61853, Riba Publishing, London (ISBN 978-1-85946-276-8)

- HSE (2006) INDG163 *Five steps to risk assessment*, 2nd edn, HSE Books, London (ISBN 0-71766-189-X)

- HSE (1998) INDG275 *Managing health and safety. Five steps to success*, HSE Books, London (ISBN 0-71762-170-7)

- HSE (2007) L144 *Managing health and safety in construction: Construction (Design and Management) Regulations 2007. Approved Code of Practice*, HSE Books, London (ISBN 978-0-71766-223-4)

- Ove Arup and Partners (2007) *Construction work sector guidance for designers*, C662, CIRIA, London (ISBN 978-0-86017-662-6)

- The Construction Confederation, *The construction health and safety manual*, Construction Industry Publications (updated regularly) <http://www.cip-bluebook.com/>.

3 Getting ready

Think ahead – what will you be doing on site?

Then:

- find out about relevant legislation and the standards it requires you to follow
- check your company policy statement and local arrangements and think how you will comply with them
- consider your own competence and training for the role you will be undertaking on site: under CDM2007 all parties must be competent for their work
- if you need training (for example you will be running a site) you must be trained for that role
- acquire any relevant health and safety qualifications – as a minimum (for a professional visiting sites) this will be the CSCS card (Construction Skills Certification Scheme)
- read relevant risk assessments and method statements
- obtain the necessary equipment, protective clothing and materials
- make sure you understand company working practices
- evaluate your need for further training.

On joining a new site, you should report to the site office and receive induction training, including site safety rules and risk assessments and method statements, and receive instructions in safety procedures:

- read the site notices
- discuss your previous safety training/experience (if any) with your immediate manager
- read the company safety policy and have the site safety organisation explained
- seek instruction on areas where you must not work alone (such as confined spaces
- be given the name and location of the safety adviser and of the on-site occupational health adviser (if there is one)
- register with a local GP (note that some sites have an arrangement with a local GP)

- find out who is the registered first-aider (this should be posted on a site notice) and where the first-aid equipment can be found
- be informed of the need to use protective clothing and equipment
- bring with you your safety equipment
- be told of your personal responsibilities for health and safety
- have explained to you the authorisation necessary for the use of plant, machinery, powered hand tools etc
- be told how to report near misses and defective plant and equipment
- see the first aid facilities
- see the site and discuss its hazards.

Most of the above information concerns the management of health and safety on the site and should be explained in the **construction phase plan.** You should read this plan and know where a copy is held if you need to refer to it. Note that it is a live document which is developed through the construciton phase.

Discuss these points with your manager or safety adviser to ensure you understand them. Ask about anything that bothers you, including hazards which concern you and which have not been mentioned.

You will also need to inform your manager of:

- any illness, disability or medication that may affect your site actions, eg colour blindness, epilepsy, diabetes or vertigo. You may need to check whether medication can cause drowsiness or vertigo etc or could influence drug testing were that required on site
- any hazards or risks associated with your work which may affect others, so that the site supervisor may be made aware and take account of them in the construction phase plan.

> **You must not come to work under the influence of alcohol or drugs or take alcohol or drugs while at work.**

3 Getting ready

Avoid working alone until you know the site layout. If you have to work alone **ALWAYS** tell your immediate supervisor:

- where you are going
- what you will be doing
- when you will be back
- that you **are** back.

Wear appropriate clothing, particularly footwear, helmet and high-visibility clothing, and tie back long hair so that it doesn't become trapped in moving parts or machinery.

- CITB, GE 707, *Safe Start*, Construction skills, (ISBN 978-1-85751-109-3)
  <http://www.citb.co.uk/publications/product.asp?p=12>

 Thousands of head injuries sustained at work are reported each year.

4 Personal protective equipment

Personal protective equipment (PPE) does not stop accidents, but it can help to lessen their effects. Employers have a duty to eliminate the hazard and/or control the risk, so far as is reasonably practicable. So PPE represents a last line of defence for the individual.

There are many types of PPE, from helmets to footwear, each type designed to protect a different part of the body against a specific hazard. This chapter explains some of the common types of PPE.

The Personal Protective Equipment at Work Regulations require the employer to ensure that everyone issued with suitable protective clothing or equipment is told:

- how to wear and use it
- the hazards against which it affords protection
- the limitations of the protection
- how to carry out any pre-use checks
- how to maintain and store it
- how to keep it clean
- to report loss, damage or deterioration immediately it is detected (including the person to report to), and to obtain replacements
- to report any problems in its use
- when to return for replacement items with a limited life
- to sign for receipt of issue and any replacement.

In addition to the equipment intended for specific hazards, there is of course general protective clothing for work in wet and cold weather, and high-visibility clothing for roadworks.

You are most at risk during your first days on site. Think and plan ahead.

Head protection

The Construction (Head Protection) Regulations 1989 require that head protection is worn when directed to do so, to comply with written site rules and at any other time that there is a risk of head injury.

If in doubt, wear your helmet

Change your helmet:

- at the manufacturer's recommended frequency, or
- after a significant impact, or
- if it becomes deeply scratched or cracked.

Do not leave your helmet in bright sunlight – this weakens the plastic.

Foot and leg protection

Safety footwear with both toe and sole reinforcement is essential on site to prevent crush injuries to your toes and to stop sharp objects puncturing the soles of your feet.

Hearing protection

Regular exposure to excessive noise causes damage to the inner ear and permanent loss of hearing. A single exposure to a very loud noise can have the same effect. Many types of ear defenders are available, from disposable earplugs to ear muffs and system helmets incorporating ear defenders. Suitable protection can be found for every situation – **WEAR IT.**

There will be occasions when you will be legally required to wear hearing protection and may be prosecuted if you fail to do so.

In Britain, tens of thousands of foot, ankle and leg injuries are sustained at work each year.

Eye protection

There are several types of eye protectors and it is important to wear the correct type to give the required protection.

Seek advice from your safety adviser about the eye protection you will need and only use if for the specified purpose.

Hand and arm protection

Gloves give protection against cuts, toxic or irritant chemicals and dermatitis, eg that caused by cement. Use barrier creams and always check you have the correct gloves to protect against the particular hazard you face. Always wash your hands before eating, drinking or smoking.

Respiratory protection

There is a wide choice of respiratory protection for dusts, gases and micro-organisms. Seek advice from your safety adviser on the appropriate type for a job. Use respiratory protection in accordance with a written method statement for a safe system of work.

Special protection

Careful selection, maintenance, certification and regular training are needed for specialist equipment including:

- compressed air escape breathing apparatus
- artificial respirators
- fall restraint/arrest equipment and safety harnesses.

Always select these with your manager or safety advisor and ensure written safe systems of work are followed, and that the requirements of the Personal Protection Equipment at Work Regulations are implemented.

> - **always obey instructions and notices to wear PPE (you should know when PPE is unserviceable and should not be used)**
> - **check that you have the right type of PPE to protect against the hazard.**

- HSE (2005) L25 *Personal protective equipment at work. Guidance on Regulations, 2nd edn,* HSE Books, London (ISBN 0-71766-139-3) <http://www.hse.gov.uk/pubns/indg174.pdf>
- HSE (2005) INDG174 *A short guide to the Personal Protective Equipment at Work Regulations 1992,* HSE Books, London (ISBN 0-71766-141-5)
- HSE (1998) L102 *Construction (Head Protection) Regulations 1989. Guidance on Regulations,* HSE Books, London (ISBN 0-71761-478-6).

5 Access/egress and working space

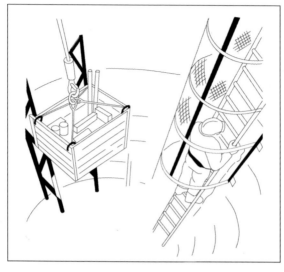

Safe access for people and their tools, equipment and materials must be provided

Ground level access/egress – follow these rules:

- all visitors (including those making deliveries) should be directed to a site access control point
- access for pedestrians and vehicles should be separated wherever possible and good visibility ensured at crossing points
- pedestrian refuges must be used where provided
- adequate lighting and signs should be provided on all access routes
- access routes for vehicles and pedestrians must be kept free of obstructions.

Access/egress above ground level

Safe access to heights must be provided by use of stairs, ladders, passenger hoists or lifts that are:

- sited away from the danger of vehicle impact
- on a stable foundation
- securely fixed and supported
- designed, erected, inspected and maintained by competent people.

 A labourer fell 3 m to his death while trying to use a roof as an unauthorised access route to a scaffold.

C669 Site safety handbook

Gangways and runways should be:

- at least three boards wide if used only by people
- at least five boards wide if used for materials access
- provided with guard rails, intermediate rails and toe boards
- less than 1 in 1½ slope.

Safety lines, harnesses, cradles and bosun's chairs should be used only by trained personnel in conjunction with a written method statement for the work, which must include fixing-point details.

Working space

CDM2007 specifically requires that a worker shall (so far as is reasonable practicable) have sufficient working space, taking account of any work equipment present. The provision of adequate working space will improve productivity as well as safety.

5 Access/egress and working space – Bibliography

- Iddon, J and Carpenter, J (2004) *Safe access for maintenance and repair*, C611 CIRIA, London (ISBN 978-0-86017-611-4)

- Lloyd, D and Kay, T (1995) *Temporary access to the workface – a handbook for young professionals*, SP121, CIRIA, London (ISBN 978-0-86017-422-6).

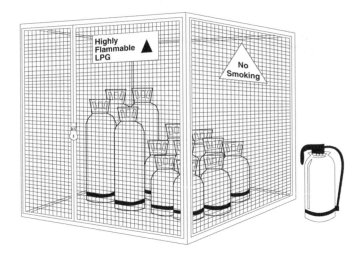

When **LPG** is used a fire extinguisher must always be available at the worksite. Staff must be instructed in emergency procedures.

Bottled gases used on construction sites include:

- liquified petroleum gas (LPG)
- oxygen
- acetylene.

All will cause fires and explosions if misused.

Always observe No Smoking signs and procedures.

 A mobile bitumen boiler overturned and set fire to two propane cylinders, which exploded, killing a 12-year-old who was playing nearby.

6 Bottled gases

You should be aware of the following safe working practices for storage, use and transport.

Storage:

- store cylinders upright in locked and secure well-ventilated labelled cages or purpose-built containers
- provide fire extinguishers nearby
- separate full and empty cylinders
- separate flammable gases from oxygen (minimum 3 m)
- site the storage cage away from buildings and excavations
- never store cylinders below ground level or in confined spaces
- never store or use an LPG cylinder in a site hut.

Use:

- ensure that cylinders are upright and cannot be easily knocked over
- check hoses, couplings and regulator for wear or damage, and ensure that flash-back arresters are used
- follow manufacturers' instructions
- always provide good ventilation
- keep bitumen boilers or similar at least 3 m from the cylinders
- return cylinders to the approved store at the end of work.

Transport:

- transport cylinders on open or well-ventilated vehicles
- secure the cylinders in an upright position
- carry an appropriate fire extinguisher
- display statutory warning notices
- ensure that drivers are trained and instructed in the hazards of carrying bottled gases.

- HSE (1999) CHI55 *Small-scale use of LPG in cylinders*, HSE Books, London <http://www.hse.gov.uk/pubns/chis5.pdf>
- LPG Association (2004) *Code of Practice 7 – Storage of full and empty cylinders and cartridges, rev edn* <http://www.lpga.co.uk/LPGA.htm>.

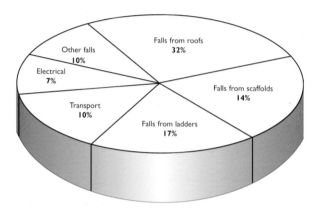

The main causes of fatalities that occur during maintenance work.
(Note: other causes contribute 10% of fatalities)

Remember: buildings may now have a health and safety file prepared for previous projects carried out in accordance with the CDM Regulations, which came into force in 1995. The file should contain information on health and safety issues and so must be consulted before planning or carrying out building maintenance work. The maintenance work itself (whether it be maintenance of the structure or of its services) will be subject to the CDM Regulations because maintenance is defined as construction work in the regulations.

It is essential inpsection and/or that maintenance work is planned and executed with the same professionalism as major works. The five major causes of maintenance deaths are shown on the pie chart on the previous page.

Everyone involved in inspection and/or maintenance work must understand the hazards and the correct procedures to minimise risk. A permit to work may be required for:

- entry into confined spaces or plant and machinery
- hot work that may cause explosion or fires
- work on pipes carrying hazardous substances or dangerous gases or their residues
- mechanical or electrical work requiring isolation of power
- roofwork over a production line
- excavation work within a factory area
- work with asbestos.

Safe access must be provided for inspection and maintenance work – see CIRIA C611 *Safe access for maintenance and repair* (Iddon and Carpenter, 2004).

Lock-off devices must be used to isolate the power supply. They must be locked off before carrying out maintenance work on or near plant and machinery etc. Permit-to-work systems must be controlled by an authorised person.

Structural stability should always be considered during maintenance and alternative means of support provided when normal supports are removed.

Building inspection work should be carried out to the same safety standards as maintenance work.

REMEMBER
- **plan the work and consider its impact on people nearby**
- **provide safe access, egress and working places**
- **use lock-off devices**
- **initiate permit-to-work systems**
- **it only takes an instant to be injured**
- **do not work alone unless it is necessary**
- **if you do work alone, follow your employers' lone working policy.**

7 Building inspection and maintenance – Bibliography

- Iddon, J and Carpenter, J (2004) *Safe access for maintenance and repair*, C611, CIRIA, London (ISBN 978-0-86017-611-4).

Asbestos is a naturally occurring mineral fibre, which is normally grey in colour. Breathing in asbestos dust can cause cancer or irreversible lung damage. The more asbestos dust you breathe in, the greater the health risk.

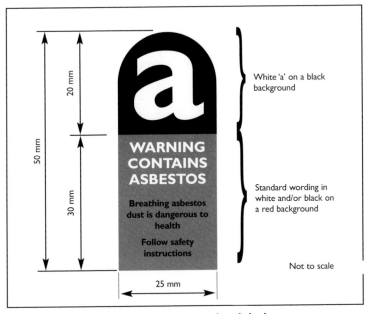

Asbestos warning label

Asbestos is a **KILLER**. It is found widely in old construction. All people in construction should be aware of it and all professionals should have received training.
See **CIRIA C670** *Site health handbook* for more details of the health risks posed by asbestos.

Although exposure to asbestos is strictly a health issue (and not an accident issue) site safety should take account of this significant risk, in particular to avoid any accidental exposure.

There is no cure for asbestos-related diseases, which kill more than 3000 people a year.

8 Care with asbestos

Asbestos may be found as:

- insulation to boilers and pipes
- fire protection of steelwork
- fire-protective cladding on doors, walls and ceilings
- roof sheeting
- floor tiles or ceiling tiles.

Any structure which has not already been surveyed for asbestos, and where there is a risk of asbestos being present, must be surveyed by an expert and an Asbestos Report prepared. Owners must also prepare a plan to manage the risk. All subsequent work (including inspections which might entail disturbance of asbestos-containing materials) must take account of that information.

Those charged with managing any intrusive inspections must always check for the potential presence of asbestos and, where it may be present, plan to avoid its disturbance.

Before any work with asbestos begins, the contractor or other employer must carry out a full assessment of the controls needed to protect workers and anyone else affected.

In many circumstances, asbestos work can only be carried out by a licensed asbestos contractor with notification to the HSE. A written plan for the work will be required in accordance with HSE guidelines and Approved Code of Practice for asbestos work.

If asbestos is suspected or in place, then leave it alone.

If in doubt, arrange for suspect materials to be laboratory-tested for asbestos. The laboratory undertaking the testing of samples must be accredited.

Do not enter an asbestos working area unless you are:

- **trained**
- **wearing appropriate PPE**
- **instructed to do so.**

- BSI, BS2501:1989, *General criteria for the operation of testing laboratories*
- HSE (1999) INDG289, *Working with asbestos in buildings*, HSE Books, London (ISBN 0-71761-697-5)
- HSE (2002) HSG 227, *A comprehensive guide to managing asbestos in premises*, HSE Books, London (ISBN 0-71762-381-5)
- HSE (2002) INDG223Rev3, *A short guide to managing asbestos in premises*, HSE Books, London (ISBN 0-71762-564-8)
- HSE (2006) *Control of Asbestos Regulations 2006, Approved Code of Practice and guidance* L143, HSE Books, London (ISBN 0-71766-206-3) <http://www.hse.gov.uk/pubns/books/l143.htm>
- HSE (2006) HSG248, *Asbestos: the analysts' guide for sampling, analysis and clearance procedures*, HSE Books, London (ISBN 0-71762-875-2)
- HSE (2006) HSG247, *Asbestos: the licensed contractors guide*, HSE Books, London (ISBN 0-71762-874-4)
- HSE (2007) INDG418, *Asbestos kills: a guide to protecting yourself*, HSE Books, London (ISBN 978-0-71766-271-5)
- HSE (2008) HSG213, *Comprehensive guidance on working with asbestos in the building maintenance and allied trades*, 2nd edn, HSE Books, London (ISBN 0-71761-901-X)
- HSE (2008) HSG 210, *Asbestos essentials*, HSE Books, London (ISBN 978-0-711766-263-0)
- HSE website: *asbestos* <http://www.hse.gov.uk/asbestos>
- HSE/TUC (2006) *The Control of Asbestos Regulations: a guide for safety representatives*, HSE Books. Download from: <http://www.hse.gov.uk/asbestos/repsguide.pdf>.

METHANOL

Toxic by inhalation and if swallowed
Keep out of reach of children
Keep container tightly closed
Keep away from sources of ignition
No smoking
Avoid contact with skin

Highly flammable   **Toxic**

200-659-6
EEC label

Supplied by
XXXXXXXXXXXXXXXX
XXXXXXXXXXXXX
XXXXXXXX
XXXXXXXXXXXX

Example of a supply label for a pure substance

AUNTIE MARY'S PATENT CLEANSER
contains trichloroethylene

Possible risk of irreversible effects
Do not breathe vapour
Wear suitable protective clothing and gloves

Harmful
1 litre

Mixed by
XXXXXXXXXXXXXXXXXXXXXXXXX
XXXXXXXXXXXX
XXXXXXX
XXXXXXXXXXXX

Example of a supply label for a manufactured preparation

The hazards

Some substances can poison you by being directly absorbed through the skin, while others cause skin problems, eg dermatitis. Dust particles entering your lungs can scar the tissue. Some dusts cause cancer. Fumes can be fatal, especially in poorly ventilated areas. Safe systems of work must be used to limit the amount of dust and fumes produced, and to limit skin contact with hazardous chemicals.

CHIPS (also known as CHIP)

CHIPS stands for the Chemicals (Hazard Information and Packaging for Supply) Regulations 2002 (as amended 2005). The objective of CHIPS is to help protect people and the environment from the ill-effects of chemicals. If you know about the chemicals you use they are less likely to harm you or the environment. These regulations are amended frequently.

CHIPS requires suppliers to:

- identify the hazards (or dangers) of the chemicals they supply – this is called classification
- inform their customers about these hazards
- package the chemicals safely.

Similar duties are placed on people who transport chemicals by road.

Suppliers' information includes:

- material safety data sheets
- clear labels on packaging that provide information in a standardised format.

The information provided should also be referred to when selecting materials to be used and available for reference to those using the materials.

Chemicals, dust and fumes can enter your body:

- by inhalation
- by swallowing
- through the skin.

Get hold of a copy of *The complete idiot's guide to CHIP*, and read it (web downloadable).

9 Chemicals, dust and fumes

These symbols appear on packaging and containers to warn of the hazards associated with their contents.

Meaning

Safety precautions and medical action

Toxic/very toxic

May cause serious health risk or even death if inhaled or ingested, of if it penetrates the skin

1. Wear suitable protective clothing, gloves and eye/face protection.
2. After contact with skin, wash immediately with plenty of water.
3. In case of contact with eyes, rinse immediately with plenty of water and seek medical advice.
4. In case of accident, or if you feel unwell, seek medical advice immediately.

Corrosive

On contact may cause destruction of living tissue or burns

1. Wear suitable protective clothing, gloves and eye/face protection.
2. Take off immediately all contaminated clothing.
3. In case of contact with skin, wash immediately with plenty of water.
4. In case of contact with eyes, rinse immediately with plenty of water and seek medical advice.

Harmful

May cause limited health risk if inhaled or ingested or penetrates the skin

1. Do not breathe vapour/spray/dust.
2. Avoid contact with skin.
3. Wash thoroughly before you eat, drink or smoke.
4. In case of contact with eyes, rinse immediately with plenty of water and seek medical advice.

Irritant

May cause inflammation or irritation on immediate, repeated or prolonged contact with the skin or if inhaled

1. Do not breathe vapour/spray/dust.
2. Avoid contact with skin.
3. In case of contact with eyes, rinse immediately with plenty of water and seek medical advice.
4. In case of contact with skin, wash immediately with plenty of water.

Highly flammable

May become hot or catch fire in contact with air or is gaseous and will ignite at any ignition source

1. Protect from source of ignition.
2. Have fire precautions at hand.

The effects may be immediate or may only appear after several years

Chemicals, dust and fumes can enter your body:

- by inhalation
- by swallowing
- through the skin.

The Control of Substances Hazardous to Health (COSHH) Regulations aim to protect workers from the effects of hazardous substances.

Hazardous substances include:

- solvents
- plaster
- fillers
- animal droppings
- concrete additives

- cement
- weedkiller
- brick dust
- micro-organisms
- ground contamination

- glues
- bitumen
- silica dust
- PCBs, eg from transformers.

COSHH requires employers to take six steps:

1 Know the substances employees (including you) may be exposed to.

2 Assess the hazard to health they can cause:
   - level of risk and degree of exposure.

3 Eliminate or control the hazard
   - use a non-hazardous alternative
   - limit the number of people exposed to the substance.

4 Inform, instruct and train employees in
   - the nature of the risk and controls to be adopted
   - reasons for using PPE
   - monitoring to be carried out.

5 Monitor the effectiveness of controls and initiate health surveillance where appropriate.

6 Keep records.

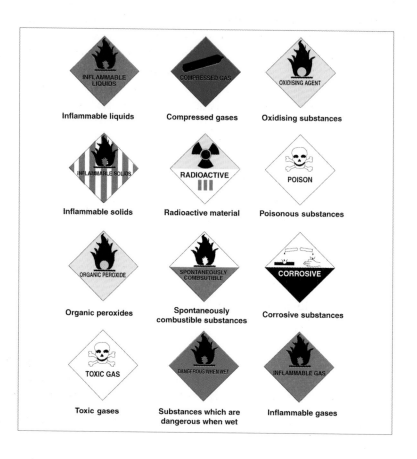

The hazard diamonds illustrated above tell you the nature of the hazard of a substance. They appear on bulk tankers and on fixed installations, eg storerooms and on packaging.

Remember that a **COSHH** assessment considers the work process, the substances involved, the risks to health and safety, who is involved and how the substance could cause harm, eg by skin contact.

Each year the HSE produces guidance document EH40, which lists the safe working limits for fumes and dust in air. As these limits are constantly reviewed and often revised it is essential that you use the current edition of EH40, using the web-downloadable version at <http://www.hse.gov.uk/coshh/table1.pdf> (note that the title which refers to 2005 omits to mention that this list is updated annually – this may be corrected shortly, however).

Your duties under COSHH are to:

- take part in training programmes
- read container labels and information sheets
- follow safe working practices and COSHH assessments
- use the correct PPE
- pay attention to personal hygiene
- store chemicals and equipment safely
- report any hazard or defect to your manager
- take part in health surveillance
- know emergency procedures.

You should be aware of the risks to third parties and the environment posed by legitimate activities, or accidents, occurring within the site, for example, wind-blown paint spray or dust, or accidental pollution of rivers and drains.

Any person using a hazardous material should be able to refer to the relevant *Material safety* data sheet (see CHIPS, page 45).

Two common site hazards, lead and asbestos, are not covered by COSHH because they have their own specific regulations. The basic points outlined above still hold true, however.

The COSHH Regulations require the identification and control of ALL hazardous substances at work.

9 Chemicals, dust and fumes – Bibliography

- HMSO (2002) SI 2002/1689, *The Chemicals (Hazard Information and Packaging) Regulations 2002* (ISBN 0-11042-419-0) and subsequent amendments

- HSE (2002) CIS26 REV2, *Cement,* HSE Books, London <http://www.hse.gov.uk/pubns/cis26.pdf>

- HSE (2002) INDG350, *The idiot's guide to CHIP,* HSE Books, London (ISBN 0-71762-333-5) <http://www.hse.gov.uk/pubns/indg350.pdf>

- HSE (2002) INDG353, *Why do I need a safety data sheet?* HSE Books, London (ISBN 0-71762-367-X) <http://www.hse.gov.uk/pubns/indg353.pdf>

- HSE (2004) HSG97, *A step by step guide to COSHH assessment,* HSE Books, London (ISBN 0-71762-785-3)

- HSE (2005) EH40, *Workplace exposure limits,* HSE Books, London (ISBN 0-71762-977-5) <http://www.hse.gov.uk/coshh/>

Confined spaces kill

Two cases illustrate the point:

> At a reservoir site four men, all aged under 30 and physically fit, died in a surface water manhole 4 m deep. Naturally evolved carbon dioxide had displaced oxygen. No tests were made before entry. The first man down collapsed and the three other men climbed down to their deaths in futile attempts to effect a rescue.

> When an engineer collapsed in a sewer, a rescuer entered without breathing apparatus and was overcome; a second person made a similar vain attempt to reach the victims. When the rescue team from the fire brigade arrived they had to remove the two would-be rescuers before they could get to the engineer. By that time it was too late and he died.

The Confined Spaces Regulations 1997 state:

"No person shall enter into a confined space unless it is not reasonably practicable to achieve that purpose without such entry".

Furthermore: "No person shall enter a confined space unless a system has been devised assessing the risks and which makes the work safe and without risk to health". Suitable emergency measures should also be in place to enable all persons to be rescued in the event of a danger to health occurring.

A confined space is "Any place including any chamber, tank, vat, silo, pit, trench, pipe, sewer, flue, well or other similar space in which by virtue of its enclosed nature, there arises a reasonable foreseeable risk".

Typical confined spaces include:

- solvents
- shafts
- tunnels
- manholes
- sewers
- box girders
- ceiling voids
- cellars and basements
- boilers and process vessels.

Confined spaces are **not** necessarily small or completely enclosed.

Even in an emergency, do not enter a confined space unless you are fully equipped to do so. If in doubt, assume the workplace is a confined space.

10 Confined spaces

The four main hazards of confined spaces are:

- suffocation – lack of oxygen (CDM2007 specifically requires that work places are supplied with fresh or purified air)
- toxic atmosphere – presence or ingress of gases, eg
  - carbon monoxide
  - hydrogen sulphide
  - nitrogen oxides
- flammable atmosphere – presence or ingress of gases, eg
  - methane
  - petrol vapour
  - town gas
- inundation – drowning.

In a confined space it may be difficult to lift and carry things, and movement generally is restricted and slowed down.

Do not enter a confined space until all the following conditions have been met:

- that work cannot be done without entering the confined space
- you are part of a trained team of sufficient number for the job
- you are working to and understand a written method statement, which preferably involves a permit-to-work control system
- all necessary atmosphere tests have been properly conducted and recorded, adequate ventilation is provided (or breathing apparatus is used) and continuous atmosphere tests will be undertaken
- plant to supply fresh or purified air has an effective device to give warning of malfunction
- you are equipped with adequate
  - overalls, gloves and footwear
  - breathing and head protection
  - safety harness, lighting and communications
- rescue arrangements and emergency procedures have been planned and you know them. Trained and suitably equipped person(s) must remain at the entrance of the confined space for the duration of the work.

- HSE (1997) INDG258, *Safe work in confined spaces*, HSE Books, London (ISBN 0-71761-442-5) <http://www.hse.gov.uk/pubns/indg258.pdf>

- HSE (1997) L101, *Safe work in confined spaces. Confined Spaces Regulations 1997. Approved Code of Practice, regulations and guidelines*, 2nd edn, HSE Books, London (ISBN 978-0-71761-405-9)

- EuroView (1999) *Health and safety: confined spaces*, Creative Channel Productions (video) <http://www.euroview.co.uk/creative.htm>.

(Note: an MEWP is a mobile elevated working platform).

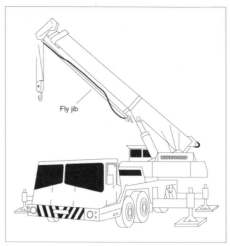
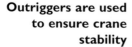

Outriggers are used to ensure crane stability

Fly jib

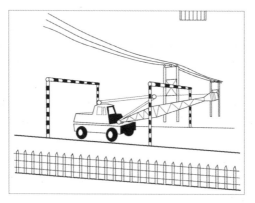

Travelling under power cables, use safety clearance goalposts

Provide at least 600 mm clearance between cranes and any obstructions

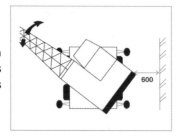

600

All equipment must comply with the Lifting Operations and Lifting Equipment Regulations 1998.

All lifting operations need to be planned and managed.

Crane access

- overall height, width and swept path of crane for delivery must be checked
- approach and working areas to be as level as possible
- ground surface to be capable of taking loads
- safe height for passage underneath power lines to be determined – by reading the marker plate underneath the wire, or by phoning the electricity company – and goal posts erected.

Crane siting

- all cranes must be sited in a stable position – consider the requirements for crane outriggers and the required ground-bearing capacity; this may require specific design of ground strengthening or temporary work
- maintain at least a **600 mm** clearance between cranes and obstructions to prevent anyone becoming trapped
- barriers to separate cranes from overhead power lines must be at a horizontal distance of at least 6 m plus jib length from the power lines. Mark the danger area with permanent stakes or flags and high-visibility tape
- when the safe working distance cannot be maintained, contact the electricity company to investigate re-routing or disconnecting the electricity supply – this may not be simple and must be planned well in advance
- when there are several cranes on site they must be sited clear of each other to prevent possible fouling of the jibs and loads
- the working area must be kept free of unnecessary obstructions and adequate lighting provided
- the crane must be a safe distance away from excavations, slopes, underground services, soft ground etc with outriggers fully extended. Use grillages to distribute the load.

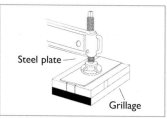

Provide grillages to distribute the force from outriggers

Protect the load and the slings by providing packs

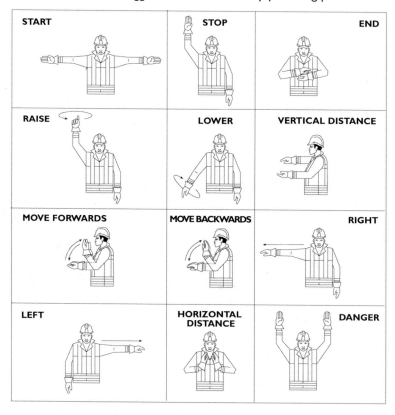

START	STOP	END
RAISE	LOWER	VERTICAL DISTANCE
MOVE FORWARDS	MOVE BACKWARDS	RIGHT
LEFT	HORIZONTAL DISTANCE	DANGER

Ensure that standard listing signals are used and that only trained banksmen are employed

Refer to the construction phase plan for the management arrangements laid down by the principal contractor for the control of lifting operations.

Crane operation

All operations must have full regard for public safety. Never lift over areas used by the public. Cranes must only be operated by trained and certificated drivers. Before starting lifting operations the driver must have documents recording the weekly inspection and the following prescribed examinations or tests:

- following any significant change or potential deterioration
- at a maximum interval of 12 months (six months if suitable for lifting persons) or as determined by the competent person
- test and thorough examination within the last four years
- inspection every six months of chains, slings and lifting gear.

These inspections and examinations must be recorded in the prescribed manner and documents must be available.

The crane must not be used if these documents are unavailable, incomplete or out-of-date.

A trained banksman (who will use only the standard signals) and trained slingers should be present. It is essential that the crane driver knows who the banksman is. An appointed person (BS 7121) must plan and monitor the lifts.

All cranes with a lifting capacity above one tonne must have an automatic safe load indicator and the weight of all loads and the lifting radii should be determined in advance of lifting. A crane must not be allowed to operate with the safe load indicator bell sounding: if it does, ensure that the crane driver stops and inform your manager.

Use tail ropes to control unwieldy loads, eg formwork or bundles of scaffold tubes. **Never use a single sling.**

Each day the crane driver should:

- inspect the whole machine including ropes, tyres and tracks, lifting gear, including chains
- check that the automatic safe load indicator and load/radius indicators are working
- put the crane through all its movements to check brake and clutch operation.

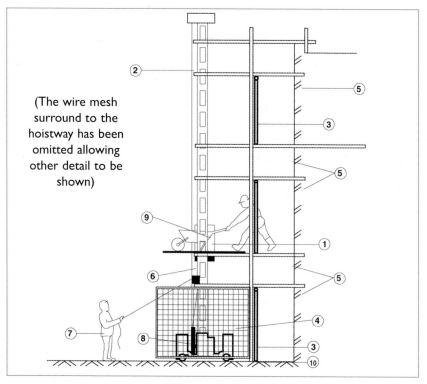

(The wire mesh surround to the hoistway has been omitted allowing other detail to be shown)

Sketch of a platform goods hoist

Safety rules for goods hoist operation

1 No passengers to be carried.

2 An over-run device must be fitted.

3 2 m high gates at landings.

4 The hoist must be enclosed appropriately.

5 The hoist mast should be tied to the structure.

6 A fall-arrester device must be fitted.

7 Operator must have clear view of whole hoist.

8 Fail-safe operating control must be fitted.

9 Safe working load must be displayed on the platform.

10 Gates to be closed before the platform is moved.

11 Hoists should only be operable from one position.

Goods hoists

There are three main hazards associated with goods hoists:

1 Falling down the hoistway.

2 Being struck by the moving platform.

3 Being hit by material falling from the platform.

Hoists must be erected, extended and dismantled only by competent, trained people. Hoist operators must be aged 18 or over and be trained to operate the hoist in question. The driver must be positioned so he can see the entire hoistway.

Follow these rules for carrying materials on hoists:

- place loose materials (eg bricks) in a container or use a hoist with a cage; tall materials must be kept within the cage
- chock wheelbarrows or other mobile plant on the platform
- ensure that the safe working load is displayed on the platform and that it is not exceeded.

The following tests and records are required:

- the safe working load must be recorded in the prescribed manner
- every week the hoist must be inspected before use, and after alteration
- a thorough examination must be undertaken as detailed in the scheme of examination prepared by the competent person.

These inspections and examinations must be recorded in the prescribed manner and documents must be available.

MEWPs (Mobile elevated work platforms)

Work at height

Under the Work at Height Regulations 2005, all situations need to be risk assessed to decide the safest way of working at height and the work process itself has to be risk assessed.

> **Never allow anyone to ride on a goods hoist. There are additional requirements for passenger hoists.**

Selection of a MEWP

In many situations a MEWP will be the safest solution, because the capability of a MEWP has been designed for safe operation. There will, however, be factors to consider, including:

- stability and support at ground level
- risks from obstructions and electricity
- risks from other vehicles
- task to be performed, including tools to be used.

Management of MEWPs

Having selected a MEWP for a task, it is necessary to evaluate risk and apply controls, including:

- avoiding potential hazards, eg by improving ground conditions
- reducing and controlling remaining risks
- ensuring operatives are informed, trained and equipped, consulting them where appropriate
- working within agreed parameters (eg permit-to-work systems)
- daily checks including weather (eg wind, ground softening) and equipment
- providing fall restraint equipment if there is any risk of impact which could cause operatives to fall.

For further information on MEWPs, see HSE information sheet MISC614

- BSI, BS 7121, *Code of practice for safe use of cranes*, Part 1 (2006), 2 (2003), 3 (2000), 4 (1997), 5 (2006), 11 (1998), 12 (1999) and 14 (2005)

- D Lloyd (ed) (2003) *Crane stability on site: an introductory guide*, 2nd edn, SP131, CIRIA, London (ISBN 978-0-86017-456-1)

- CPA (2001) CIG 0701 *Working at height on mobile cranes – best practice guide*

  □ HSE (1998) SS13, *Construction goods hoists*, HSE Books, London (now withdrawn)

  □ HSE (1991) CIS19, *Safe use of mobile cranes on construction sites*, HSE Books, London (now withdrawn)

- HSE (1996) L64, *Safety signs and signals. The Health and Safety (Safety Signs and Signals) Regulations 1996. Guidance on Regulations*, HSE Books, London (ISBN 0-71760-870-0)

- HSE (1998) L113, *Safe use of lifting equipment. Lifting Operations and Lifting Equipment Regulations 1998. Approved code of practice and guidance*, HSE Books, London (ISBN 0-71761-628-2)

- HSE (2003) MISC614, *Preventing falls from boom-type mobile elevated working platforms*, HSE Books, London

- Iddon, J and Carpenter, J (2004) *Safe access for maintenance and repair*, C611, CIRIA, London (ISBN 978-0-86017-611-4)

- Lloyd, D and Kay, T (1995) *Temporary access to the workface – a handbook for young professionals*, SP121, CIRIA, London (ISBN 978-0-86017-422-6)

- TSO (1998) SI No 2307, *The Lifting Operations and Lifting Equipment Regulations 1998*, HMSO, London (ISBN 0-11079-598-9).

12 Demolition and dismantling

Demolition and dismantling work is particularly hazardous. It should only be carried out by competent and experienced demolition contractors.

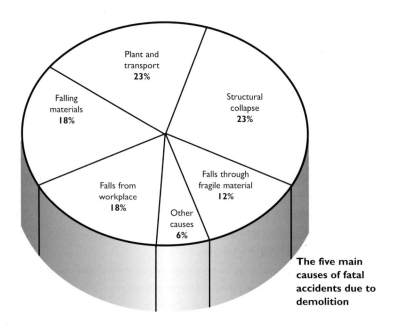

The five main causes of fatal accidents due to demolition

If in doubt about the stability of a permanent or partly demolished structure, consult a structural engineer.
Always check with your manager if you are concerned.

There are three main types of demolition or dismantling:

- by mechanical means
- by explosives
- by hand.

Demolition is often high-risk and should be closely supervised and carefully planned.

Do not enter demolition sites without first getting permission from both the person in charge and your manager.

Key points include:

- safe distances from the structure must be established to eliminate the hazard of debris falling on workers or the public during explosive demolition of a factory chimney or multi-storey block
- the public and workers must be protected from falling materials by the use of properly constructed boarded fans. Fans are for protection only. Do not use them for access, stacking or storage of materials
- safe places of work must be provided, complete with guard rails and toe boards. When these cannot be provided, safety harnesses must be used. Mobile access platforms are preferred
- temporary struts and guy ropes must be securely anchored and clearly marked or flagged.

 Tens of people die in demolition accidents in Britain every year.

12 Demolition and dismantling

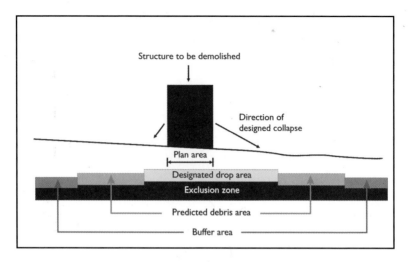

Establishing exclusion zones when using explosives in demolition

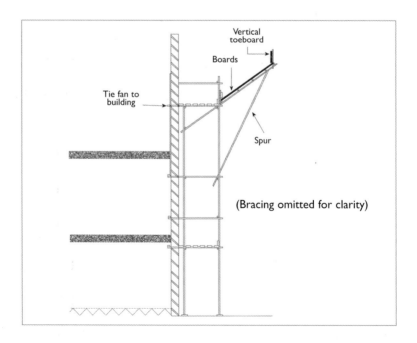

Protective fan

Before demolition or dismantling work starts

CDM2007 requires that arrangements for carrying out demolition or dismantling are recorded in writing before the work begins. The arrangements should include:

- clear management responsibilities
- lines of communication
- method statements detailing safe methods of work derived from risk assessments of the site-specific issues

Such arrangements and method statements will address at least the following:

- a competent person in charge of the operation must be nominated in writing
- a competent person must inspect the structure
- particular attention must be paid to hazardous substances. If asbestos is found, it must be removed by a licensed contractor
- information about the building structure should be obtained
- the health and safety file must be consulted where one exists
- the utility companies must be contacted and all services disconnected or diverted
- existing floors that are to be used as working platforms must be suitable for that purpose
- all necessary shoring, lighting, signs etc must be planned and the work carried out at the correct time
- suitable PPE must be provided and used during operations.

During operations:

- adequate protection and safe access for the public and workers must be provided at all times, including protection from dust and noise hazards
- all the employees must be competent for this work
- all machines must be suitable, robust and placed in safe working positions on suitable ground
- overloading of existing floors (or any part of the structure) must not be permitted. If any sign of weakness that might lead to structural instability is detected refer it to your manager immediately.

12 Demolition and dismantling – Bibliography

- BS6187:2000 *Code of practice for demolition*
- HSE (1995) CIS45, *Establishing exclusion zones when using explosives in demolition*, HSE Books, London <http://www.hse.gov.uk/pubns/cis45.pdf>
- HSE (2006) HSG150, *Health and safety in construction*, 3rd edn, HSe Books, London (ISBN 978-0-71766-182-4)
- HSE HSG29, *Parts 1 to 4 Health and safety in demolition work* (now withdrawn)
- Institute of Demolition Engineers, Orchard WR, *Elements of risk and safety management in demolition dismantling projects*
- Lloyd, D and Kay, T (1995) *Temporary access to the workface – a handbook for young professionals*, SP121, CIRIA, London (ISBN 978-0-86017-422-6)

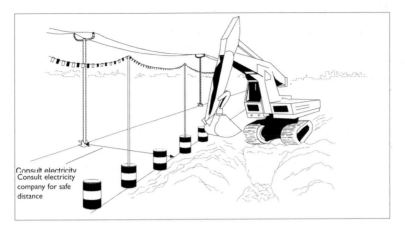

Consult electricity
company for safe
distance

Safe working near overhead power lines requires a separation zone

There are many electrical hazards on a typical site, eg:

- overhead power lines and cables
- buried cables
- power tools
- energised installations in partly completed structures.

There is no safe voltage. Even a small shock can startle you and cause you to jump back causing a slip or fall. All electrical equipment should be considered dangerous.

Voltage	Sheathing colour
25	Violet
50	White
110–130	Yellow
220–240	Blue
318–415	Red
500–750	Black

Guidance on voltages is given by the sheathing colour

 300 workers suffer major injuries from electric shock in Britain each year.

13 Electricity

Overhead/underground cables

Consider the location of overhead and underground cables at the planning stage of a project. Overhead wires are not insulated. Electricity can jump air gaps and current can be induced in metal structures parallel to power lines.

The precise position of buried cables must be determined from utility plans, confirmed using cable locators and hand digging and clearly indicated. Electric cables do not lie in straight lines, they snake about within a trench. These rules should be followed:

- risk assess underground services before undertaking any work in the ground and prevent risks so far as is reasonably practicable
- consult the electricity company to arrange diversions, isolation, or permit-to-work arrangements
- exclude vehicles etc from areas where there is a risk but no work is planned
- erect clearly marked barriers to protect overhead power lines that remain live – provide 6 m minimum clearance or as directed by the electricity company, taking account of vehicles involved
- report any damage to the insulation of underground cables to the electricity company.

Electricity distribution and use on site:

- use portable, battery-powered electric tools or voltages of 110 V maximum, unless prior arrangements have been agreed with your manager
- do not use home-made extension cables, multi-way adaptors or domestic 13 amp plugs
- repairs to electrical equipment must be by competent persons
- check the condition of plugs, leads, power tools and controls
- use the correct leads and sockets for the voltage supplied
- check that fuses are of the correct rating
- ensure temporary electrical systems are properly installed and tested
- plan for regular inspection and maintenance of all distribution systems, power tools and electric appliances
- use residual current devices (earth leakage circuit breakers) at the point of supply for 240 V hand-held equipment
- maintain a register of electrical equipment and use it to plan and record testing of equipment (max three months for 110 V equipment, monthly for 240 V equipment).

- HSE (1988) SS6, *Portable electric tools and equipment*, HSE Books, London
- HSE (1995) HSG141, *Electrical safety on construction sites*, HSE Books, London (ISBN 0-71761-000-4)
- HSE (1997) GS6Rev, *Avoidance of danger from overhead electric power lines*, HSE Books, London (ISBN 0-71761-348-8)
- HSE (2004) HSG107, *Maintaining portable and transportable electrical equipment*, 2nd edn, HSE Books, London (ISBN 0-71762-805-1)
- HSE (2000), HSG47, *Avoiding danger from underground services*, revised, HSE Books, London (ISBN 0-71761-744-0).

14 Environment

Although environmental issues affect health and not site safety per se, environmental issues can have severe immediate impact and accidental exposure to pollution should be avoided so far as is reasonably practicable.

Protection of the environment both off and on site from pollution due to site activities must be controlled at all times.

Know your local environment! Are there hospitals, schools, day centres, old peoples' homes or residential projects adjacent to your site that may be put in danger by site activities?

The main forms of pollution emissions from sites are:

- contaminated land   –   disturbance, excavation, removal

- waste disposal   –   transport, fly-tipping, burning, bonfires

- air   –   fumes, gases, dusts, vapours

- water various   –   direct or indirect discharge of various substances, effluents, spillages to drainage systems, rivers or estuaries

- noise   –   mechanical plant and equipment, transport, explosive blasting, piling, hammering.

The main hazards and contaminants that cause danger to human health are:

Hazard	Contaminants
Toxic by ingestion	heavy metals, phenols, coal tars, cyanide
Toxic by skin contact	oils, tars, phenols, asbestos, cement and other dusts/hazardous materials
Toxic by inhalation	hydrogen sulphide and other gases
Risk of explosion or fire	various gases and flammable or combustible materials

Prevention is better than cure.

Main causes of contamination from site activities may occur as a result of:

- leaks and spillages from tanks, containers and pipes/hoses either during transport, storage use or disposal
- disposal of waste materials from site
- vapour or gaseous emissions from spraying or burning
- demolition of buildings containing contaminated material, eg asbestos lagging or claddings, sealants, lead in old paint, toxic waterproofing materials on or in floors, walls and ceilings
- movement and/or migration of contaminated groundwater.

What should you do?

- check if an environmental assessment has been carried out for the development. If so, familiarise yourself with the details of any health and safety related issues
- read any site-specific procedures that have been prepared
- check COSHH assessment for hazardous material
- check that wastes are being properly segregated, controlled and disposed of
- read *Waste Management – The Duty of Care. A Code of Practice*
- if in doubt, consult your site safety officer.

There are three environmental agencies operating in the UK.

England and Wales

    Environment Agency

Scotland

    Scottish Environmental Protection Agency (SEPA)

Northern Ireland

    Department of Environment (Northern Ireland).

14 Environment – Bibliography

- Chant-Hall, G, Charles, P and Connolly, S (2005) *Environmental good practice on site – pocket book* C651, CIRIA, London (ISBN 978-0-86017-651-0)

- Charles, P, Connolly, S and Chant-Hall, G (2005) *Environmental good practice on site* (second edition) C650, CIRIA, London (ISBN 978-0-86017-650-9)

- Guthrie, P and Mallett, H (1995) *Waste minimisation and recycling in construction – a review*, SP122, CIRIA, London (ISBN 978-0-86017-428-8)

- HMSO (1990) *Environmental Protection Act 1990* (ISBN 0-10544-390-5)

- HMSO (1991) *Water Resources Act 1991*, (ISBN 0-10545-791-4)

- HMSO (1992) SI 1992/339, *The Trade Effluents (Prescribed Processes and Substances) Regulations 1992* (ISBN 0-11023-339-5)

- HMSO (1992) SI 1992/588, *The Controlled Waste Regulations 1992* (ISBN 0-11023-588-6)

- HMSO (1995) *Environment Act 1995* (ISBN 0-10542-595-8)

- HMSO (1996) *Waste Management – The Duty of Care. A Code of Practice* (ISBN 0-11753-210-X)

- HMSO (1998) SI 1988/819, *The Collection and Disposal of Waste Regulations 1988* (ISBN 0-11086-819-6)

- HMSO (2002) 12002/1559 *Landfill (England and Wales) Regulations 2002* (ISBN 0-11042-370-4)

- HMSO (2005) SI 2005/1643, *The Control of Noise at Work Regulations 2005* (ISBN 0-11072-984-6)

- HMSO (2002) SI 2002/2677, *The Control of Substances Hazardous to Health Regulations 2002* (ISBN 0-11042-919-2)

- HMSO (2005) *Hazardous Waste (England and Wales) Regulations 2005*

- HMSO (2005) *List of Waste (England) Regulations 2005*

- HMSO (2007) *Environmental Permitting (England and Wales) Regulations 2007*

- HMSO (2008) *Site Waste Management Regulations 2008*

- Renger, M et al (1994) *Environmental assessment*, SP96, CIRIA, London (ISBN 978-0-86017-379-3)

- The Water Act 2003 (ISBN 978-0-10543-703-1)

- Venables, R et al (2000) C512 *Environmental handbook for building and civil engineering projects, 2000. Part 1: design and specification* (ISBN 978-0-86017-512-4), C528, *Part 2: construction phase* (ISBN 978-0-86017-528-5), C529, *Part 3: demolition and site clearance* (ISBN 978-0-86017-529-2), CIRIA, London.

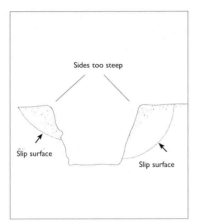

Failure by ground rotation in soft clays

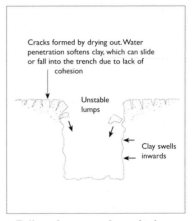

Failure by ground cracks in stiff clays

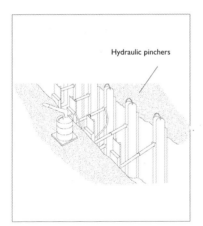

Use hydraulically-operated shoring devices in preference to timber

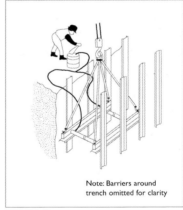

Work outside the trench whenever possible

No unsupported excavation can be considered safe, however shallow.

15 Excavations

No ground can be considered totally stable: the ground may be inherently weak, laminated or have been disturbed previously.

Water may create instability in excavations. This can occur through:

- the action of rainwater
- changes in groundwater conditions and seepage
- erosion by water
- frost action
- drying out of soil.

It is essential that all excavations are made safe by:

- having sides battered to a safe angle of repose, or
- providing structural supports, eg trench sheets and struts, drag boxes, sheet piling or proprietary systems.

Shallow trenches may not require support if the ground is firm, provided that proper safety procedures exist and are always carried out. All trenches must either have their sides adequately supported or be battered back to a safe slope.

Where ground and support arrangements allow, install the supports before excavation to final depth. The excavation and support installation should proceed by steps until final depth is reached. Adopt safe working practices, use proprietary systems which can be installed from outside the trench or work progressively forward from existing supports.

 In a typical year, eight people die in sudden excavation collapses in Britain.

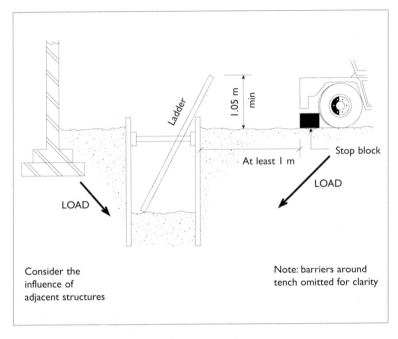

Protect the trench

Before work starts

All excavation work must be planned. Before digging begins on site, check that arrangements have been made to:

- locate underground services – check with all utility companies, look for indicator posts, valve covers and evidence of trenching, use cable and pipe detectors and/or ground radar, and (where necessary) dig trial pits
- establish ground conditions and design an adequate support system
- consider the interaction of proposed excavations and existing structures:
  - will the excavation destabilise existing structures?
  - do the existing structures have adequate foundations?
  - has the ground already been disturbed?

- acquire all available information about the ground, buried services, adjacent structures etc

- provide support to trench sides where there is any risk of collapse; options include established solutions (see CIRIA publication R97), proprietory systems such as boxes, used in accordance with manufacturer's instructions and specially designed earthwork support systems (as temporary works)

- provide edge protection for all excavations, use projecting trench sheets or other solid barriers where possible. If a person could fall more than 2 m, suitable barriers must be provided

- ensure the person directly supervising the work is fully experienced and competent in the support of excavations

- obtain the necessary drawings or sketches

- brief and instruct operatives

- provide site security, particularly in relation to preventing children getting on to the site

- establish adequate working space for plant and for spoil heaps (spoil heaps and materials should not be less than 1 m from the edge of the excavation)

- construct bridges or gangways as required

- provide sufficient ladders secured against movement

- assess need for lighting

- issue appropriate protective clothing and equipment

- protect the public (including handicapped or blind people)

- control traffic

- consider if fumes could collect in excavations.

REMEMBER
An excavation is a type of "confined space" and information given in Chapter 10 of this guidance is relevant.

During the work

A competent person must inspect the excavation and its supports at the start of each shift and after significant change, eg accidental earth fall or storm, to address the following questions:

- is access to and from the workface sufficient and secure? Access/egress should be via a staircase or a properly installed and maintained ladder
- are all working faces secure, wedges tight and support material free from damage?
- is there any sign of movement or deflection in the support system?
- is the soil condition as predicted? If not, what action should be taken?
- are spoil heaps an adequate distance back from the trench edge?
- are pipes, bricks and other materials, plant etc well clear of the edge so that there is no risk of them falling into the trench or of vibration causing danger to the support?
- are services that cross the trench properly supported?
- is there a safe system for installation of support?
- is the method statement being properly followed in installing the support? (This is particularly important in relation to the spacing of walings and struts)
- are regular tests for gases or fumes being carried out? Is ventilation required?
- has the risk of flooding or foul air been properly assessed?
- where pumping is necessary, is a proper watch being kept to ensure that fine material is not being drawn out from behind the support system?
- is resuscitation equipment available and a nominated person trained to use it?
- have all persons been instructed in evacuation procedure and the correct rescue procedure to follow if someone is overcome by gases or fumes in the trench? Is the necessary equipment installed (preferable) or to hand?
- are operatives wearing safety helmets? Is any other protective equipment needed?

- is the work adequately protected and marked during the day? Is it fenced, or covered, and lit at night? Are watchmen needed?
- are gangways over the excavation safe? Have access bridges for plant and vehicles crossing the excavation been designed by competent persons?
- are vehicle stop blocks in position?
- are vehicles/plant too close to the excavation?
- is there an agreed system of support withdrawal and have those carrying it out been properly instructed?

An inspection must also be made at the start of each work shift and a record made at least once a week.

An inspection must also be made after any fall of earth or rock, or after any other event that may have affected the excavation stability.

Alterations to planned buried service routes and the precise location of existing buried services must be recorded on as-built drawings. These are essential records for the owner/operator/maintainer of any structure, and accurate as-builts are an essential part of information required for any health and safety file.

Workers must be fully-informed about the system being used and must understand how:

- to instal new protection safely
- to minimise the time spent in an excavation
- to stay within the protected area (for example where boxes are used).

 A man was crushed when a trench collapsed. The trench was 1.9 m deep and was being dug by hand. No supports were available on-site.

- HSE (1999) HSG185, *Health and safety in excavations – be safe and shore,* HSE Books, London (ISBN 0-71761-563-4)

- Irvine, D J and Smith, R J H (1992) *Trenching practice,* 2nd edn, R97, CIRIA, London (ISBN 978-0-86017-192-8)

- Puller, M (2003) *Deep excavations: a pratical manual,* 2nd edn, Thomas Telford, London (ISBN 0-72773-150-5)

- TRADA (1990) *Timber in excavations,* 3rd edn, TRADA (ISBN 0-90134-881-3)

- Trenter, N A (2001) *Earthworks: a guide,* Thomas Telford, London (ISBN 0-72772-966-7).

16 Falling from height

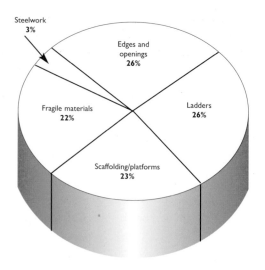

The workplaces from which construction workers fall to their deaths

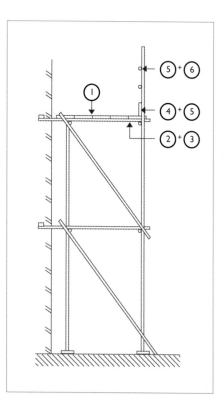

Preventing falls from an independent tied scaffold

See checklist – opposite

Scaffolds should be designed, erected, altered or dismantled only under the supervision of a competent person and by competent and experienced workers. Scaffolds should be inspected weekly by a competent person and the inspection recorded.

Does your scaffold adequately meet the requirements to reduce the risks of falling?

Check these points as a guide for traditional scaffolds:

1 Platform three to five boards wide, depending on use.

2 Each scaffold board on a working platform to have at least three supports – to be determined by strength of board, normally between 1.2 m and 1.5 m apart. This should be identified on the board strappings.

3 Scaffold boards either tied down or overhanging each end support by at least 50 mm but not more than four times the thickness of the board.

4 Guard rails and toe boards along the outside edge and at the ends of any working platform from which people or materials could fall. Use guard rails and toe boards at inside edge to prevent people or tools/materials falling.

5 Toe boards at least 150 mm high, with no more than 470 mm between the top of the toe board and the guard rail or between guard rails.

6 Top guard rail at least 950 mm above the platform.

See also chapter on *Scaffolding* for further details on towers and scaffolding.

 In a recent five-year period there were 383 construction deaths by falling.

16 Falling (from roofs)

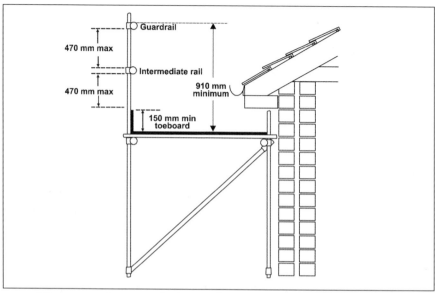

Edge protection on a sloping roof using tube and fitting scaffolding

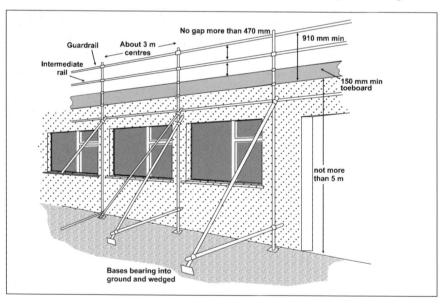

Edge protection on a flat roof using tube and fitting scaffolding

For all work on roofs, risk assessments must be prepared together with method statements and brought to the notice of those who may be at risk.

The main hazards include:

- falls from flat or sloping roofs
- falls through fragile roofs
- falls from ladders or scaffolds.

To minimise the risks, follow these rules:

- be aware of the precautions to be followed when working at heights
- display prominent permanent warning notices at the approach to any fragile roof
- never walk on fragile materials such as asbestos cement, plastics, GRP or glass. Beware – they may have been painted over or covered with insulation or dirt
- always use a planned means of access such as crawling boards or a proprietary system
- on a flat roof make sure that the edge is protected by a parapet and/or guard rails and that the roof is strong enough to support you
- where someone could fall over the edge of the roof, guard rails and toe boards must be installed or anchorage points for safety harnesses provided. Make sure that safety harnesses are worn
- prevent items falling onto people below – use brick guards, toe boards and warning notices
- keep off roofs in bad weather, eg high winds (especially if carrying sheet materials) or where there may be other hazards such as fumes or ice.

When working above ground level there is no automatically safe height, always assess the situation.

An engineer fell 4 m while descending a ladder. He was advising on the renovation of a balcony. A fully boarded out scaffold had been erected and he gained access by a ladder, which was not secured but was footed by an assistant. Unfortunately, when the engineer came to descend he did not check that the assistant still had the ladder footed securely. The assistant was caught unawares, the base slipped and the engineer fell onto the pavement.

Designing for access:

Under the Work at Height Regulations 2005, all situations need to be risk assessed to decide the safest way of working at height and the work process itself has to be risk assessed.

Falling from a ladder is a significant risk and wherever possible access should be designed as stairs, which may be temporary or may be part of the permanent structure which is designed for early installation and use.

Always follow these rules when using ladders:

- secure ladders against slipping when possible by tying at the top. A second person standing at the foot to prevent slipping is effective only with ladders less than about 5 m long. For longer ladders use stakes etc

- ladders should extend approximately 1 m above the landing place or the highest rung in use, unless an alternative hand-hold is available

- arrange ways of carrying tools and materials up and down so that both hands are free to grip the ladder

- use a ladder stay or similar device to avoid placing ladders against a fragile support, eg plastic gutters

- never place ladders where there is danger from moving vehicles, overhead cranes or electricity lines

- ensure that ladders have level and firm footings – never use unsteady bases such as oil drums, boxes, planks or tower scaffolds

A demolition worker tripped over a pneumatic hose and fell 4.6 m while working at an open edge on a demolition site.

A foreman fell 3 m from the edge of a floor. The guard rail had been removed so that he could use a power float. After the accident an alternative method of fixing the guard was devised so that the float could be used effectively.

A bricklayer tripped over a pile of asbestos sheets lying on his working platform. He fell 3.3 m head first over the edge to his death. Toe boards and guard rails had been removed and not reinstated.

- do not support ladders on their rungs
- extending ladders should overlap at least three rungs
- set ladders at a slope of 4 to 1
- provide a suitable platform in ladder runs taller than 9 m
- check ladders regularly for defects – never use damaged or home-made ladders. Take damaged ladders out of use.

Remember:

- keep all working places and access routes tidy and free of tripping hazards
- provide top guard rails at least 910 mm high and toe boards at least 150 mm high with no gap more than 470 mm (see page 82)
- provide adequate lighting
- clearly sign incomplete or dangerous scaffolds and working platforms and prevent access
- devise, implement, monitor and review safe systems of work whenever falling is a hazard
- openings of any type through which people can fall should be provided with a secure cover and marked appropriately, or guard rails provided.

Falling is the greatest single cause of death on construction sites.

16 Falling – Bibliography

- HSE (1998) HSG33, *Health and safety in roof work*, HSE Books, London (ISBN 0-71761-425-5)
- HSE (1999) INDG284, *Working on roofs*, HSE Books, London
  - ☐ HSE (1985) *Deadly maintenance. Roofs – a study of fatal accidents at work*, HSE Books, London
- National Access and Scaffold Confederation (NASC) guidance documents SG4 and TG20 (see <http://www.nasc.org.uk>).

**The symbol shows the three
conditions for fire – remove
any one and the fire will stop**

Flammable liquids on construction sites

Look for this symbol on container labels:

and for these warnings:

- flammable
- highly flammable
- keep away from sources of ignition
- no smoking.

 Approximately 300 people suffer serious burns on British construction sites each year.

17 Fire

Each year there are many fires on construction sites resulting in injuries to people and damage to property.

CDM2007 requires provisions for the prevention and control of emergencies, including fire.

This includes:

- emergency routes and exits
- evacuation procedures
- where necessary, fire detectors, alarm systems and fire-fighting equipment.

HS G168 *Fire safety in construction work* gives extremely useful guidance covering:

- how to stop fire occurring
- reducing ignition sources
- general fire precautions
- emergency procedures.

The Fire Prevention Association's publication *The joint code of practice for the prevention of fires on construction sites* is also useful and includes:

- advice on separation between accommodation units and between them and the permanent works
- fire prevention and detection methods
- standards for wrappings and coverings
- standards for sheeting to scaffolds.

Further information about scaffold cladding materials and materials to be used in construction are provided in the Loss Prevention publication LPS1215 Requirements for the *LPCB appraisal and listing of scaffold cladding materials* and LPS1207 *Fire requirements for the LPCB approval and listing of protective covering materials.*

(Note: LPCB stands for the Loss Prevention Certification Board, now administered by the BRE).

 Fire precautions are particularly important during refurbishment and maintenance work.

C669 Site safety handbook

The information sheet CIS51, *Construction fire safety* (HSE, 1997) is useful for construction projects with lower fire risks such as low-rise housing developments. Fire precautions and emergency arrangements should be included in the construction phase plan.

Suitable emergency routes and exits must be provided, signed and kept clear. Emergency lighting for these routes should be provided where risk assessment indicates this to be necessary.

Details of permanent emergency systems, eg sprinkler systems and fire alarms, must also be included in the health and safety file.

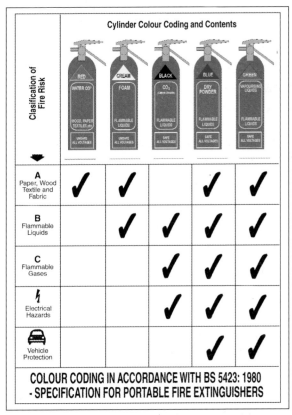

Fire extinguishers made after May 1996

Fire extinguishers made before May 1996 are entirely coloured according to the coding shown above, ie water extinguishers were red, foam extinguishers were cream and so on.

17 Fire

Fire prevention is much better than fire fighting:

- flammable waste must be stored tidily prior to disposal
- do not burn rubbish on site
- flammable materials must be stored away from hazardous processes, eg welding, fabrication areas
- all flammable material stores must have warning signs
- petrol-driven plant must be switched off before refuelling and a funnel used to avoid splashes
- smoking must be prohibited within 6 m of flammable liquid and gas cylinders, No Smoking signs prominently displayed and good ventilation provided
- heating and cooking appliances must be properly installed
- many fires are caused by carelessness in drying wet clothes over fires/heaters.

Hot work, eg burning and welding, requires special consideration:

- consider use of hot work permits
- remove combustible material to beyond the area of sparks and spatter, or provide flameproof protection
- do not use tarpaulins as protection against sparks
- the work site must be checked after the hot work is completed, as fires can smoulder for hours.

Adequate fire-fighting equipment, fire detectors and doors must be provided. Site personnel must know:

- the correct types of extinguisher and their location, their colour code and limitations of use
- how to use the extinguishers provided.

Each site must have a fire emergency plan. All persons must know what that plan is and the part they play in it.

- Fire Protecion Association (2006) FSB9-6, *Fire prevention on construction sites*, 6th edn (ISBN 0-90216-739-1)

- HSE (1996) INDG227, *Safe working with flammable substances*, HSE Books, London (ISBN 0-71761-154-X) <http://www.hse.gov.uk/pubns/indg227.pdf>

- HSE (1996) HSG140, *Safe use and handling of flammable liquids*, HSE Books, London (ISBN 0-71760-967-7)

- HSE (1997) CIS51, *Construction fire safety*, HSE Books, London <http://www.facelift.co.uk/health-safety/media/Construction%20Fire%20Safety-CIS51.pdf>

- HSE (1997) HSG168, *Fire safety in construction work*, HSE Books, London (ISBN 0-71761-332-1)

- HSE (2008) HSE8Rev, *Take care with oxygen. Fire and explosion hazards in the use and misuse of oxygen*, 2nd rev edn, HSE Books, London <http://www.hse.gov.uk/pubns/hse8.pdf>.

18 Frame erection

Mobile access plant should be used whenever possible.

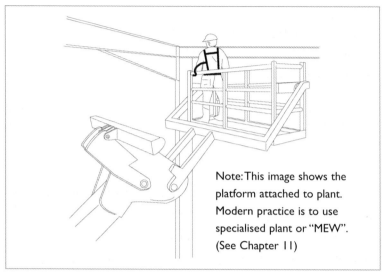

Note: This image shows the platform attached to plant. Modern practice is to use specialised plant or "MEW". (See Chapter 11)

Telescopic hydraulic work platform in use for steel erection

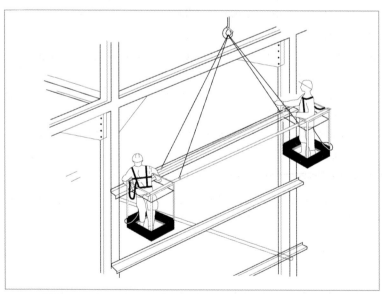

Using a sheeting rail cradle to provide safe access

There are four main hazards associated with frame erection:

- falling
- being struck by falling tools or materials
- collapse of the partly erected structure
- adverse weather conditions.

Consideration of safety during frame erection should start at the design stage and be carried through by means of a written method statement for the site work.

Design stage – consideration should include:

- options for prefabricated assemblies prepared off-site or at ground level
- stability during all stages of erection of the structure
- the effect of the erection sequence on stability
- assessment of loading at all stages of construction, including temporary loads due to erection
- safe means of connecting components including safe access and working places – consider using remote handling where possible
- safe handling, lifting and transportation
- recognition of the practical problems of the steel erector, eg access to make connections
- incorporation of landing brackets or other aids to safe erection such as bolted on lifting shackles
- incorporation of edge protection for later stages of construction.

The procedure for the erection of very heavy or complex members should be explained by designers in the pre-construction information.

A design team member may also be required on site during steel erection to ensure there is no misunderstanding about the intended safe erection procedure.

Keep out of the area of frame erection unless it is absolutely necessary to be there. Obtain the erection supervisor's permission before you enter the area.

18 Frame erection

CIRIA publication SP121 *Temporary access to the workface* provides more detailed guidance on safe access procedure for frame erection including:

- mobile elevated working platforms
- telescopic boom equipment
- man-riding skips and cradles
- abseil access techniques.

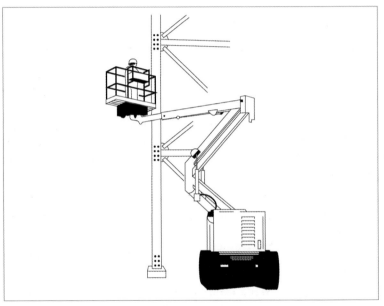

Self-propelled articulated boom

A safe system of work for frame erection should be set down in the method statement.

 Wear a safety harness in telescopic boom access machines.

Erection stage – the method statement should include:

- scheme management and co-ordination, responsibilities and authority of personnel at all levels and the provision and maintenance of effective communication

- erection sequence

- slinging strategy including the use of bolt on shackles, quick-release hitches and other devices to reduce manual intervention and reduce overall risk

- methods of ensuring stability at all times (including overnight) of individual components (including columns) and sub-assemblies, as well as partially erected structures

- a detailed method of erecting the structure and an erection scheme devised to ensure that lifting, initial connecting, unslinging, and final connecting are carried out safely

- procedures for work in adverse weather conditions, eg high winds and wet weather

- measures to prevent falls from height such as safe access and safe places of work. These may include special platforms and walkways, mobile towers, mobile access plant, slung, suspended or other scaffolds, secured ladders, safety harness, safety nets and supervision to ensure that all equipment is properly used

- provision of barriers such as screens, fans and nets for protection from falls of material and tools

- provision of suitable plant (including cranes) and tools and equipment of sufficient strength, capability and quantity

- contingency back-up in the event of breakdown of essential plant and equipment

- delivery, stacking, movement on site and on-site fabrication or pre-assembly

- details of site features, layout and siting of offices and stores, with notes on how these may affect proposed erection procedures.

18 Frame erection – Bibliography

- BCSA (2004) 36/04, *Code of practice for erection of low rise buildings* (ISBN 0-85073-044-9) <http://www.steelconstruction.org/static/assets/source/Low-Rise%20book.pdf>

- BCSA (2006) 42/06, *Code of practice for erection of multi-storey buildings* (ISBN 0-85073-051-1)

- HSE (1984–1986) GS28, *Safe erection of structures* (in four parts), HSE Books, London (ISBN 0-11883-530-0)

- Lloyd, D and Kay, T (1995) *Temporary access to the workface – a handbook for young professionals*, SP121, CIRIA, London (ISBN 978-0-86017-422-6).

Two simple ways to reduce the risk of manual handling injuries on construction sites

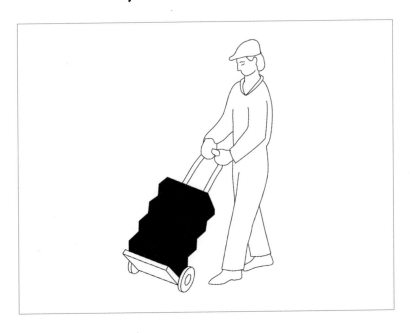

19 Manual handling

More than 25 per cent of all reported injuries involve manual handling.

The Manual Handling Operations Regulations apply to:

- lifting
- carrying
- reaching
- pushing
- pulling
- twisting.

Employers are required to:

- avoid manual handling where reasonably practical, eg use mechanical equipment
- assess potentially hazardous manual handling that cannot be avoided
- implement measures to reduce the risk of injury as far as possible.

Designers can contribute to reductions in manual handling risks, eg by:

- designing in good access for plant, equipment and materials
- considering manual handling during future maintenance
- careful specification of materials, eg building blocks and bagged products.

Organise delivery and stacking/storage of materials to minimise lifting and carrying.

Keep block and bag sizes to a minimum, eg order smaller bags of plaster. For all awkward or heavy loads, a risk assessment must be prepared. If in doubt – ask to see it.

Rules for lifting

- bend your knees, not your back
- keep your back straight, lift with your legs and look where you are going
- keep the load close to your body
- avoid twisting.

The HSE's MAC tool may be used (see: <http://www.hse.gov.uk/msd/mac/index.htm>.

Back injuries are the greatest single cause of absence from work.

19 Manual handling

Size up the job

- are the floors sloping, slippery or greasy?
- are there obstructions or stairs?
- if the object is too heavy to lift, get help
- know where the object is to be put down.

Stand firmly

- stand close to the load
- place your feet about 0.5 m apart
- place one foot in front of the other in the direction of movement.

Bend your knees

- keep your back straight
- keep your chin well in.

Get a firm grip

- use the whole of your fingers – not just the finger tips
- keep the load close to your body
- grip boxes diagonally.

Lift with your legs

- lift by straightening your legs
- keep your back straight
- use the impetus of the lift and start moving off in the required direction.

Putting things down

- keep your back straight
- bend your knees
- don't trap your fingers
- put the load down askew and slide it into place.

Always use mechanical aids for lifting heavy and awkward objects. Get help when necessary.

- HSE (1994) HSG115, *Manual handling. Solutions you can handle,* HSE Books, London (ISBN 0-71760-693-7)
- HSE (1999) CIS37, *Handling heavy building blocks,* HSE Books, London
- HSE (2004) L23, *Manual handling. Manual Handling Operations Regulations 1992 (as amended). Guidance on Regulations,* 3rd edn, HSE Books, London (ISBN 0-71762-823-X) <http://www.hse.gov.uk/lau/lacs/56-1.htm>
- HSE (2004) INDG143Rev2, *Getting to grips with manual handling. A short guide,* 2nd edn, HSE Books, London (ISBN 0-71762-828-0) <http://www.hse.gov.uk/pubns/indg143.pdf>
- HSE (2006) AS23Rev3, *Manual handling solutions for farms,* 3rd edn, HSE Books, London (ISBN 978-8-071766-186-2) <http://www.hse.gov.uk/pubns/as23.pdf>.

Sound pressure in decibels	Situation	Sound pressure in pascals
	Peak action level, immediate irreversible damage	200
140	– Jet at 30 m	100
130	– Threshold of pain	
	– Pneumatic breaker (unsilenced) at 1 m	
120	– Pneumatic digger	10
	– 600 HP scraper at 2 m (pass by)	
110	– Rock drill	
	– Diesel hammer driving sheet steel at 10 m	
100	– Scabbling	
	– 7 HP road roller on concrete at 10 m	1
95	– Concrete pouring	
90	– Second action level	
	– Drilling/grinding concrete	
85	– First action level	
80	– Scaffold dismantling at 10 m	0.1
	– 8 HP diesel hoist at 10 m	
70		
	– 5 HP power float at 7 m	
60		0.01
	– Typical office	
50		
	– Living room	

Typical sound intensities

Facts about noise

- sound pressure is measured in decibels (dB). The decibel scale is logarithmic and it doubles with every increase of 3 dB, ie 78 dB is twice as loud as 75 dB and 81 dB is four times as loud
- the effect of noise on the hearing is cumulative and irreversible
- whenever possible, limit noise at source.

The Control of Noise at Work Regulations 2005 require:

- whenever possible, limit noise at source
- evaluate the risk of workers being exposed to excessive noise
- provide personal protection
- monitor workers and keep risks under review.

Exposure to high levels of noise over extended periods will damage your hearing. Noise-induced hearing loss is irreversible.

Loud noises can cause:

- permanent damage to hearing
- your hearing to become less sensitive
- permanent ringing in the ears
- breakdown of safe and effective communication.

If, with normal hearing, you have difficulty conducting a normal conversation at 1 m, the background noise level is about 90 dB; difficulty at 2 m means the noise level is about 85 dB. Move away!

The Noise at Work Regulations require employers:

- to assess noise levels
- at the **First Action Level of 85 dB(A)** to provide employees with information about the risks to hearing and provide hearing protection on request
- at the **Second Action Level of 90 dB(A)** to control noise exposure by:
  - limiting the noise at source, as the first step
  - requiring hearing protection to be worn
  - limiting the time people are exposed to noise
- at the **Peak Action Level of 200 pascals** (equivalent to 140 dB(A)) to control noise exposure. The Peak Action Level is relevant to single loud noises and can cause instantaneous hearing damage, eg use of cartridge tools in an enclosed space.

Using environmental legislation, local authorities have the power to serve notices that specify noise levels, limit working hours for noisy operations, or ban certain types of machines if complaints are received.

If you are served with such a notice...

CONTACT YOUR MANAGER IMMEDIATELY.

When you are in a hearing protection area, wear your ear defenders all the time; removing ear defenders for only half an hour in eight hours reduces the overall protection afforded by 40 per cent.

- BSI (1997) BS 5228-1:1997, *Noise and vibration control on construction and open sites. Code of practice for basic information and procedures for noise and vibration control*

- Ferguson, I (1995) CRR73, *Dust and noise in the construction process*, HSE Books, London (ISBN 0-71760-768-2)

- HSE (1998) INDG99, *Noise at work. Advice to employees*, HSE Books, London (ISBN 0-71760-962-6) <http://www.hse.gov.uk/pubns/indg362.pdf>

  □   HSE website search "noise" <http://www.hse.gov.uk/>

- HSE (2005) L108 *Controlling noise at work. The Control of Noise at Work Regulations 2005. Guidance on Regulations*. HSE Books, London (ISBN 0-71766-164-4)

- HSE (2005) INDG362Rev1, *Noise at work. Guidance for employers on the Control of Noise at Work Regulations 2005*, HSE Books, London <http://www.hse.gov.uk/pubns/indg362.pdf>

- HMSO (2005) SI2005 No.1643, *The Control of Noise at Work Regulations 2005*, The Stationery Office (ISBN 0-11072-984-6)

- Waller, R A (1990) *Planning to reduce noise exposure in construction*, TN138, CIRIA, London (ISBN 978-0-86017-317-5)

- Wills, A J and Churcher, D W (1999) *How much noise do you make? A guide to assessing and managing noise on construction sites*, PR70, CIRIA, London (ISBN 978-0-86017-870-5).

General

All pressure tests must be conducted in accordance with a written method statement, which must include the risk assessment and necessary control measures.

Before pressure testing begins, the following must be checked for damage, correct alignment, jointing integrity and compatibility:

- pipes
- valves
- fittings and flange connections
- pipeline restraints.

Pressure testing must not be carried out until all these are correct.

Pipes and fittings should be checked to ensure that they are designed to pass the pressure test plus allowable overload.

Whenever practicable, hydraulic pressure testing should be used. Air is 20 000 times more compressible than water and the sudden release of a large volume of compressed air is in effect an explosion. Use pneumatic testing only when hydraulic testing is unacceptable.

At the pressure ranges normally encountered, the amount of energy stored in compressed air or gas is 200 times that contained in water at the same pressure and volume.

Do not exceed maximum test pressure.

All pressure testing, if not carefully controlled, can be dangerous. Sudden release of uncontrolled pressure acts like an explosion and can kill and maim. Three men died in such an explosion.

21 Pressure testing

Hydraulic testing

- people working in the area should be warned before hydraulic tests begin
- before a test starts, ensure that all anchorages are in position, that concrete anchorages are adequately designed for test pressure and have developed the required strength, and that the backfill between the pipe body and the trench side is well compacted
- air valves or suitable tappings should be located at appropriate high points of the main to allow the air to escape while the pipe is being filled. If the pipeline is on a level grade, it may be necessary to bleed air off at several points to ensure complete evacuation. After the air has been evacuated, all vent holes must be plugged
- where the joints of buried pipelines are to be left uncovered until testing has been completed, sufficient backfill material should be placed over the body of each pipe to prevent movement
- each section to be tested should be properly sealed off with special stop ends designed for the safe introduction and disposal of the test water and release of air
- stop ends should be secured by adequate temporary anchors. The thrust on the stop ends should be calculated and temporary anchors designed accordingly
- the section under test should be filled with clean water, taking care that all air is displaced. Where the pipeline will be used for carrying potable water, the water used for testing should be clean and disinfected.

Never use oxygen, propane, acetylene or any flammable gas to pressure-test pipelines.

C669 Site safety handbook

- BSI (1998) BS EN 752-4:1998, *Drain and sewer systems oustide buildings. Part 1: Generalities and definitions (1996) Part 2: Performaance requirements (1997) Part 3: Planning (1997) Part 4: Hydraulic desiign and environmental considerations* (1998)
- HSE (1998) GS4, *Safety in pressure testing,* 3rd edn, HSE Books, London (ISBN 0-71761-629-0).

22 Public safety and site security

Major causes of fatalities to the public arising from construction work and lapses of site security are:

- being struck by falling objects
- falling from height
- being struck by moving plant or equipment
- falling into holes and drowning or being crushed (particularly children)
- hazards present in partially completed work. Many injuries are caused by tripping over unexpected obstacles.

Children

- construction sites are a magnet to children
- wherever possible, arrange for a company safety officer to visit local schools to warn of construction site dangers
- consult HSE guidance for further precautions to be taken.

Storms

When high winds are forecast and before every site shutdown (eg Christmas) pay particular attention to:

- scaffolding, ie check ties, sheeting, bracing, boards and all connections and foundations
- stability and security of boundary fences
- storage including sheet materials and waste materials, eg empty chemical containers
- stability of lighting towers, cranes, hoardings and all temporary works.

Arrangements to protect public safety must be included in the health and safety plan.

C669 Site safety handbook

General

All employers have a general duty under Section 3 of the Health and Safety at Work etc Act to take reasonably practicable measures to minimise risks to the general public.

These include:

- secure site fences wherever practicable. Display warning signs and keep access gates locked outside working hours to prevent unauthorised access
- safety zones to separate the public from construction works. This is particularly important for roadworks and multi-storey works in city centres. In such cases the highway authority must be consulted
- sites that cannot be fenced off should have high-visibility barriers, warning signs and adequate lighting and security staff as appropriate
- material must never be thrown or dropped from a height in an uncontrolled way
- securely support and guard all excavation to limit public access – provide lighting and secure fencing for these areas
- material deliveries and site activities (eg scaffold tube hoisting) to be organised to avoid lifting operations over roads and pavements open to the public. If such lifting is unavoidable, arrange diversions and/or closures
- mobile plant and equipment is to be immobilised when it is not in use. Small plant, bottled gases and chemicals are to be securely stored in their approved places
- construction operation in public areas must cause minimum disruption to pedestrians and road users.

CDM2007 requires a principal contractor to take reasonable steps to ensure only authorised persons are allowed on site and specifically requires that the site perimeter is identified by suitable signs and/or fenced off, depending on the level of risk.

 One member of the public is killed by construction activities every two months on average.

- HSE (1997) HSG151, *Protecting the public – your next move* HSE Books, London (ISBN 0-71761-148-5).

Refurbishment work is construction work and needs to be planned and managed in the same way as all other construction work. However there are special considerations:

- any of the hazards discussed in this handbook may apply on a refurbishment site, sometimes for only a brief period, so they may not get proper attention
- much refurbishment work is fragmented and requires skill and application to manage effectively
- the work may be messy, bitty and difficulty, so workers need to keep alert and not take chances
- sites often get messy and then dangerous due to a greater risk of slips, trips and falls
- normal practice such as edge protection may be forgotten in the rush of events
- there may be a significant risk of finding the unexpected – including asbestos containing materials (ACM)
- there may be a significant risk from uncontrolled demolition/dismantling which is carried out in an ad hoc manner and with periods when there are (perhaps only temporarily) stability issues
- premises being refurbished may often remain partially occupied, creating further hazards
- who is in overall control of the work from the point of view of strength and stability? Have written procedures been prepared? (as required in CDM2007)
- are suitably competent people and organisations involved for all aspects of the work?

In 2007 more than half of all construction fatalities occurred during refurbishment work. During a blitz on refurbishment sites during early 2008, the HSE served prohibition notices on a disgracefully high 30 per cent of the sites visited. Particular issues identified were:

- working at height in an unsafe manner (a major concern)
- equipment which was broken and/or not being used properly
- unprotected edges and openings
- cluttered surfaces which were unsafe to walk on (bad housekeeping, untidy sites)

- obstructed walkways and stairs
- workers not briefed on how to work safely.

Much refurbishment work is small and involves a large number of small teams and individuals who operate independently, sometimes without proper overall site management and control – which is illegal under CDM2007. If you see this happening, you should report your concern.

Much refurbishment work is small and involves a large number of small teams and one-man-bands who operate independently, sometimes without proper overall site management and control – which is illegal under CDM2007. If you see this happening, you must report your concern.

- Fawcett, W and Palmer, J (2004) *Good practice for refurbishing occupied buildings*, C621, CIRIA, London (ISBN 978-0-86017-621-3)

- James, D (2006) *Building adaptation*, 1st edition, Butterworth-Heinemann (ISBN 978-0-75065-085-4)

- Lazarus, D, Bussell, M and Ross, P (2003) *Retention of masonry façades – best practice guide*, C579, CIRIA, London (ISBN 978-0-86017-579-7)

- Loughborough University and Milan Polytechnic (2004) *Health and safety in refurbishment involving demolition and structural instability*, HSE Report RR204 <http://www.hse.gov.uk/research/rrpdf/rr204.pdf>

- Riley, M and Cotgrave, A (2005) *Construction technology 3: the technology of refurbishment and maintenance*, Palgrave Macmillan, Hants (ISBN 978-1-40394-095-7).

There are two main hazards associated with both mobile and fixed scaffolding:

- people and/or materials falling from the scaffold
- overturning or collapse of the scaffold.

Chapter 16 deals with falling off a scaffold. This chapter deals with precautions against scaffold collapse or overturning.

Tower scaffolds

- the scaffold is to be erected and used in accordance with the manufacturer's instructions and the safe working load restrictions are to be observed

- the tower must rest on a firm base on level ground. Use the outriggers and ensure the castors are locked before the tower is used

- the ratio of height to least base dimension should not normally exceed 3:1 for outside work, or 3.5:1 for inside work, unless tied to suitable fixed points, but see manufacturer's recommendations

- use internal ladders/stairs for access to the working platform. Never use the scaffold framework as a ladder unless it is purpose-designed. Separate ladders should be used only where the design of a tower permits

- tower scaffolds must not be used outside during winds of force 4 or greater unless securely tied

- the tower is to be securely tied to the structure whenever it is to be used for grit-blasting, heavy drilling, or it is to be sheeted out

- overhead power lines and obstructions must be considered when constructing, using or moving the tower

- the tower must never be moved with people or materials on the working platform

- the tower must only be moved from the base

- once the move is completed the outriggers must be re-engaged and the castors locked

- should not be used unless they have been inspected by a competent person at the start of each shift.

Someone dies every month dies in a scaffolding accident on British construction sites.

24 Scaffolding (fixed)

This section applies to conventional tube and fitting scaffolds although most of the points made apply to proprietary equivalents. Reference on detailed matters may be made to BSEN 12811 and guidance proposed by the NASC (National Association of Scaffolding Companies).

Support the standards on a secure base

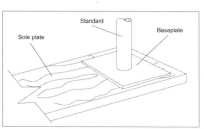

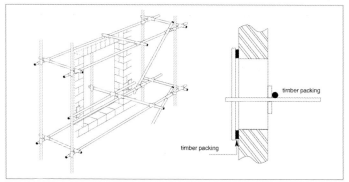

A through tie

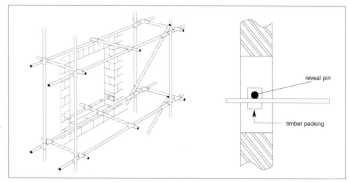

A reveal tie

Removal, renewal or alteration of ties should be carried out only by a competent scaffolder.

Under the Work at Height Regulations 2005 all situations need to be risk assessed to decide the safest way of working at height and the work process itself has to be risk assessed.

For fixed scaffolding the following points need to be borne in mind:

- scaffolds must be designed. This may be achieved by working within parameters set out in the NASC's guidance SG20:05, or by a full structural design or by the use of proprietary scaffolding systems
- ties must be tested in accordance with NASC guidance G4:04.

> **Design of scaffold systems (either design to NASC guidance or a full structural design) requires specialist knowledge and experience.**

24 Scaffolding (fixed)

For scaffolding to be safe, it must be stable and designed to take the anticipated load. This depends on a secure base, a suitable height in relation to its mean base dimension or being tied to a permanent structure to prevent movement. Detailed advice follows.

Base

- level wooden sole plate (positioned from outside to inside standard) surmounted by steel base plate with central spigot to prevent displacement of the standard
- daily check to ensure no undermining, slippage or settlement.

Standards (upright tubes)

- must be vertical with staggered joints made by internal expanded fittings.

Ledgers (running longitudinally parallel to the structure)

- joined by externally placed clamp (sleeve coupler) staggered to ensure joints do not fall in the same bay
- ledger secured to standards with right-angle couplers (load-bearing).

Transoms (tubes placed on ledger at right angles to the structure)

- these complete the square of scaffolding and are used as supports for boards
- there must be a transom provided adjacent to every standard joined with right-angle load-bearing couplers
- intermediate transoms provided to support boards may be joined with wrap-over fittings (non-load-bearing).

Ledger brace

- a tube running diagonally from upper front to lower rear ledger in alternate bays of scaffolding
- load-bearing couplers must be used
- may run from standard to standard (use load-bearing swivel coupler)
- may all run in same direction or in reverse of each other (dog-leg bracing).

Longitudinal facade or face brace

Fitted from base to top of scaffold at a diagonal across the face to prevent bowing of the face or sway movement.

Ties

Ties must be provided to secure the scaffold to the structure. Only 50 per cent of ties in a scaffold may be reveal ties.

- through tie – a tie assembly through a window or opening in a wall
- reveal tie – tube placed into window reveal with screw fitting
- box tie – made by encompassing column or outer part of permanent structure
- drilled anchorages – female part fitted to suitably sound part of the structure, male part attached to scaffold to tie to the building
- where ties do not prevent inward movement this must be done by abutting the transoms to the face of the building
- ties must not be fitted to external decorative fittings, eg downpipes or balustrades.

24 Scaffolding (fixed)

Working platforms

Must be even and fully boarded – width depends on usage of scaffold.

Toe boards and guard rails

Required on all working platforms, access ways, stairways and landings, where a fall of more than 2 m is possible.

Access to working platforms

Access normally by ladders or stairways. Ladder must be tied and at an angle of 4:1.

Loading

Loading should be vertically above the standards where possible or at specially strengthened loading bays.

NOTE: The wall thickness of scaffold tubes can vary – eg UK tube is thicker than European tube – so load-bearing capacities can vary. Tubes of different thicknesses or of different metals (eg steel and alloy) should not be mixed in a designed structure.

REMEMBER
No scaffold – fixed or mobile – should be used unless it has been inspected by a competent person:
- **at the start of each shift and a report prepared within the previous seven days**
- **after exposure to adverse weather conditions that may have affected its strength or stability**
- **after any substantial modification or alteration.**

All inspections must record the prescribed information.

- BSI (2004) BS EN 12811-1:2003, *Temporary works equipment. Performance requirements and general design*
- CITB (2005) CE 509, *A guide to practical scaffolding,* 4th edn, CITB (ISBN 978-0-90202-991-0)
- HSE (1997) CIS49, *General access scaffolds and ladders*, HSE Books, London
- HSE (2005) CIS10Rev4, *Tower scaffolds*, 4th edn, HSE Books, London <http://www.hse.gov.uk/pubns/cis10.pdf>
- Lloyd, D and Kay, T (1995) *Temporary access to the workface – a handbook for young professionals*, SP121, CIRIA, London (ISBN 978-0-86017-422-6)
- TG 20:05 NASC <http://www.nasc.org.uk/>.

25 Site investigation and remediation

Initial survey

Before going to site consider the hazards you may encounter.

These can include:

- surveying on live roads
- contaminated land
- dilapidated buildings
- confined spaces

- old cellars, walls or shafts
- unstable ground or pits
- live services
- asbestos.

Consider which hazards you may meet and how they could affect you. Assess the risks, plan ahead by recording what control measures you will put in place and stay alert to risks while on-site.

Site investigation

Drilling and digging trial pits may expose the ground investigation team to hazards including:

- contaminated land – COSHH assessments required
- collapse of ground
- methane (or other gas) pockets – the agreed safe system of work must include gas detection, testing and emergency procedures
- underground services.

The following general rules apply to site investigation:

- there should be a minimum of two drilling crew per rig
- never enter an unsupported trial pit
- appropriate lighting, barriers and warning signs must be provided
- particular attention must be paid to site security at the end of each working day
- staff must wash their hands before eating or drinking
- eating, drinking and smoking should only be allowed in designated clean areas, eg site welfare facilities
- adequate storage must be provided for dirty or wet clothing and PPE.

Existing services include:

- overhead and underground electric and telephone cables
- water
- sewerage
- gas
- chemical pipelines
- cable TV.

Standard colour codes are increasingly being adopted for services. See downloadable guidance from the National Joint Utilities Group. However coloured markings should not be relied upon.

All services present hazards. The first essential move towards avoiding danger from overhead or underground services is to contact the local offices of the relevant company – British Telecom, British Gas, electricity, water and cable companies and highway authorities. Obtain as much information as possible about the location of cables, lines and pipes. Thereafter, it is important to maintain close liaison with the companies as long as the work is in progress.

Erect goalposts and barriers to protect overhead services and use cable locators to pinpoint the location of underground services.

After use of locators (by trained personnel), trial holes should be carefully dug, using hand tools, to confirm the position of buried services.

Once underground services have been located it is important to identify them correctly. Consult the service companies for confirmation and to record their location, type and depth permanently. Ensure the health and safety file is updated with these records.

Site remediation

Site remediation work must be planned and executed in a similar manner to other construction work and may involve a variety of processes covered by other sections in this handbook. Many points relevant to site investigation will also apply to subsequent remediation work.

> **The use of hand-held power tools and mechanical excavators too close to underground services is a major cause of accidents.**

- British Drilling Association (1992) *Guidance notes for the safe drilling of landfills and contaminated land*

- BSI (1999) BS 5930:1999 *Code of practice for site investigation*

- HSE (2000) HSG47 *Avoiding danger from underground services,* HSE Books, London (ISBN 0-71761-744-0)

- ICE (1993) *Guidelines for the safe investigation by drilling of landfills and contaminated land,* Thomas Telford, London (ISBN 0-72771-985-8)

- IGEM (2002) IG/SR/18 Edition 2 *Safe working practices to ensure the integrity of gas pipelines and associated installations*

- National Grid website <http://www.nationalgrid.com/uk/>:

  ☐　　*Excavating safely – general advice*

  ☐　　*Excavating safely – avoiding injury when working near gas pipes*

- Rudland, D J and Jackson, S D (2004) *Selection of remedial treatments for contaminated land. A guide to good practice,* C622, CIRIA, London (ISBN 978-0-86017-622-0).

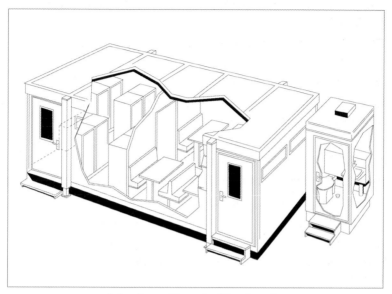

A basic welfare facility for sites

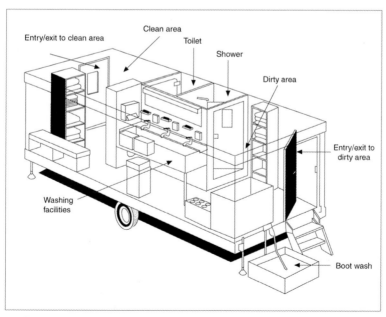

Clean area

Entry/exit to clean area

Toilet

Shower

Dirty area

Entry/exit to dirty area

Washing facilities

Boot wash

A good standard of hygiene facility for contaminated sites

26 Site set-up and cleanliness

Site organisation

Health, safety and welfare standards are reinforced by the early provision of:

- adequate canteen, hygiene and first-aid facilities and toilets
- a secure perimeter fencing to the site
- clearly defined site access and vehicle routes
- vehicle washing facilities
- all necessary PPE and adequate storage space for PPE
- clearly defined storage, office and working areas
- emergency procedures and statutory notices posted in highly visible places
- a mobile phone until fixed phones are installed.

Notify the emergency services of site location, activities and access.

Major sites should have a fully equipped first-aid room, but every site must have:

- cleanser, towels and clean hot water for washing
- at least one first-aid box
- small portable first-aid kits for people who do not have easy access to the first-aid box.

First-aid boxes should have a list of contents inside the lid.

Your company must provide an adequate number of fully trained first-aiders or appointed persons, who must be readily identifiable.

Site cleanliness

CDM2007 specifically requires that a site shall, as far as is reasonably practicable, be kept in good order, with work areas kept in a reasonable state of cleanliness and, in particular, that timber or other material with projecting nails (or other projecting sharp objects) must not be used in the works and must be cleared away if it could be a risk to people.

All employees should receive site induction training including details of the site layout, site rules and emergency procedures. Visitors should always be accompanied. Do not enter a site alone without first informing others.

CDM2007

CDM2007 contains the standards for welfare facilities on construction sites. Schedule 2 of the Regulations sets out the welfare facilities required including:

- sanitary conveniences (toilets) and fully-equipped washing facilities at readily-accessible places
- drinking water and cups
- changing rooms, lockers and clothes-drying facilities
- heated rest areas, water and arrangements for preparing and eating meals.

Facilities must be kept in a clean and orderly condition and be provided for use throughout the duration of on-site works.

Work conditions

CDM2007 specifically requires:

- adequate room to work
- adequate temperature and weather protection
- adequate lighting and (where necessary) emergency lighting.

Each of these requirements will affect the risk of accidents happening.

26 Site set-up and cleanliness – Bibliography

- HSE (1998) CIS18REV1, *Provision of welfare facilities at fixed construction sites,* HSE Books, London <http://www.hse.gov.uk/pubns/cis18.pdf>.

The correct PPE must be used with small plant

Small plant and equipment:

- affects others working nearby
- must be used only by competent personnel
- must be kept clean and well maintained
- must have all guards fitted and effective
- can create noise and dust
- may vibrate
- requires the wearing of appropriate PPE
- should be kept in locked stores when not in use. Stores must be clean, dry, well lit and well ventilated, and have an issue/recovery control system
- fuels should be kept and transported in suitable, properly labelled containers.

 20 per cent of all construction fatalities occur as a result of accidents with mobile plant and equipment.

27 Small plant and equipment

All small plant and equipment is potentially dangerous.

Small plant and equipment frequently involved in accidents includes:

- saws
- cartridge-operated fixing tools
- abrasive wheels
- compressed-air tools.

Cutting, drilling, grinding, punching or sawing with small plant is dangerous. There is also a risk of damage to the human body due to noise and vibration. These risks are addressed by the Control of Noise at Work Regulations 2005 and the Control of Vibration at Work Regulations 2005 (which has ACoP L140 dealing with hand-arm vibration), which require that limits to exposure to noise and vibration are set, that cumulative exposure is monitored and that appropriate protection is provided.

All plant and equipment must meet the requirements of the Provision and Use of Work Equipment Regulations. These regulations place duties on employers to:

- ensure that equipment is suitable for its intended use
- consider the working environment when choosing equipment, eg waterproof, robust equipment for outdoor use, or intrinsically safe electrical equipment for use in sewers
- maintain equipment in good order
- train and inform staff in the use of work equipment, including how to perform daily checks and report defects.

 The Regulations require that exposure to noise and vibration is assessed; that, if possible, it is avoided and that the residual risk is minimised and actively managed.

There are also specific duties placed upon the employer to:

- guard dangerous machinery parts, eg circular saw blades
- provide adequate lighting in which to use the equipment
- ensure controls are working and easy to use, and that there are no "home-made" modifications
- provide a means by which equipment can be isolated from all power sources for maintenance or adjustment
- protect workers from machinery parts at high or very low temperatures, eg ground-freezing plant.

Where training is required before operating tools or equipment, it should normally be certificated so that an employee can prove that they have been trained. Examples of equipment requiring certificated training include:

- cartridge tools
- chain saws
- abrasive wheels
- burning equipment.

Maintenance

All plant and equipment requires regular maintenance.

Daily checks are part of these procedures and should be monitored to ensure they are done.

Examples of daily checks on chain saws

- stop switch – works
- guide bar and sprockets – not broken
- chain brake – works
- lubrication system – full.

27 Small plant and equipment – Bibliography

- AFAG, leaflets on chainsaws 301–310
  <http://www.aie.org.uk/resources/aie_pub_afag.html>
- HMSO (1998) SI1998 No. 2306 *The Provision and Use of Work Equipment Regulations 1998*, TSO, London (ISBN 0-11079-599-7)
- HSE (2005) L140, *Hand arm vibration – the Control of Vibration at Work Regulations 2005*, HSE Books, London (ISBN 0-71766-125-3)
- HSE (2005) L141, *Whole Body Vibration. The Control of Vibration at Work Regulations 2005. Guidance on Regulations*, HSE Books, London (ISBN 0-71766-126-1).

Surveying and setting-out work may be part of construction work and needs to be planned and managed in the same way as all other construction work. If it is not part of construction work, hazards and risks need to be assessed and managed in any event. The following special considerations should be borne in mind:

Risk management

- a site specific risk assessment should be made before starting work and when circumstances change

- any necessary control measures should be identified and the work should be properly planned and managed. Training may be needed

- on a live construction site, surveying work should be planned and executed in consultation and under the direction of the principal contractor

- on occupied premises, surveying work should be planned and executed in consultation and under the direction of the premises manager

- even for as brief piece of work, information about the site must be ascertained (see *Getting ready*)

- surveying on live roads requires special expertise: involve experts and consult with the relevant authorities concerning issues such as road closure, lane closure, timing, signing, lighting, speed limits

- surveying on railways requires special expertise: involve experts and consult with the relevant authorities concerning issues such as possessions, permits, reporting and liaison, lookouts and PTS (personal track safety) training.

Hazards

- any activity in the area being surveyed may present a hazard to the surveyor – consult with the person responsible
- many of the hazards discussed in this guide may apply and the relevant sections should be consulted (eg working at height)
- surveyors should be alert for issues such as live overhead lines, exposed electrical wires etc, asbestos (in whatever form, including dust in ceiling cavities etc), rough ground, uneven or slippery floors, hidden voids or rotten covers, unstable structures, rubbish – sharps, needles, glass etc, high winds, projecting nails, hazardous substances, contamination, noise issues such as traffic noise etc (see also the RICS publication *Surveying safely – your guide to personal safety at work*)
- surveyors should be familiar with issues associated with their equipment, such as lasers and manual handling of heavy or awkward equipment, particularly in confined spaces or when ascending ladders
- at remote sites there may be a lack of easy access for emergency services; what would happen if there was an accident?
- surveying may involve working in confined spaces or working alone; precautions should be taken after the risks have been assessed
- when surveying on live roads, the traffic hazard may involve impact from straying vehicles if the work causes obstruction or distracts drivers or if a surveyor loses concentration and walks into the traffic. The effects of turbulence from large vehicles upon people and equipment may also need to be considered.

> **Surveying and setting out sound like safe activities – but anyone working in a construction environment or in an environment such as a live road is at risk**

- Building Surveying Faculty (2005) *Building surveys and inspections of commercial and industrial property,* 3rd edition, RICS Books, Coventry (ISBN 978-1-84219-193-4) <http://www.ricsbooks.com/productInfo.asp?product_id=7858>

- Gibson, D, Hanney, N, Rushforth P, Smith S, Walsh, C and Workman, G (2008) *Surveying and engineering: principles and practice,* Wiley-Blackwell and ABE (ISBN 978-1-40515-923-4)

- HSE (2005) *The Work at Height Regulations*

- RICS (2006) "Your guide to personal safety at work" free web download In: *Surveying Safely,* **2,** Aug, Royal Insitution of Chartered Surveyors <http://www.enetosh.net/files/17/SurveyingSafely.pdf>

- RICS *Surveying safely* (<www.rics.org>)

- Sadgrove, B M (2007) *Setting out procedures for the modern built environment,* C709, CIRIA , London (ISBN 978-0-86017-709-8).

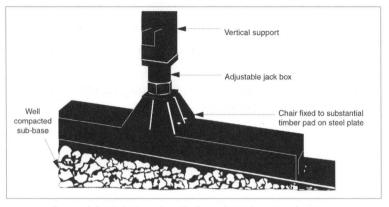

A good foundation details for a load bearing base

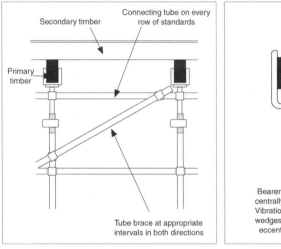

Bracing

Bearers

A temporary works co-ordinator should be appointed before work begins. He will be responsible for checking and signing for each stage of the works.

Temporary works include:

- falsework and formwork
- cofferdams and their bracing systems
- temporary supports to unstable structures
- temporary bridging
- scaffolding
- support to excavations
- temporary electrical supplies.

Design

- all temporary works must be designed by competent people
- calculations, drawings and sketches to explain and illustrate the temporary works design must be produced
- an independent design check should be carried out also considering any effects on the permanent works.

Method statement

A written method statement for construction and use of the temporary works is essential. It must include:

- the name of the person in charge
- detail of the design and loading limitations
- construction details and erection and loading sequence
- a specification for plant, materials and methods to be used
- details of supervision, inspection and checks to be made
- design tolerances, eg deflection/elongation
- any formal permits to load or dismantle that are required
- striking times and sequence
- dismantling sequence.

Method statements must detail health and safety arrangements.

Structural strength

Regardless of the need or otherwise for temporary works, the strength and stability of new or existing structures must be maintained throughout the works. Assessment of strength and stability must include consideration of condition and loading during the works.

There must be no unauthorised departure from temporary works design or method statements. Authority must only be given in writing by the temporary works designer (co-ordinator).

29 Temporary works and structural strength – Bibliography

- Bragg, S L (1975) *Final report of the Advisory Committee on Falsework, (The Bragg Report)*, HMSO, London

- BSI (2004) BS 5975, *Code of practice for falsework*, 1996 (amended 2004)

- HSE (1987) HSG32, *Safety in falsework for in-situ beams and slabs*, HSE Books, London (ISBN 0-11883-900-4)

- HSE (2003) CIS56, *Safe erection, use and dismantling of falsework*, HSE Books, London <http://www.hse.gov.uk/pubns/cis56.pdf>.

Never hitch a lift on mobile plant

Avoid working close to plant and equipment whenever possible

 Every year many people are killed or injured on site by reversing vehicles.

30 Vehicles, machinery and site transport

Large mobile plant and machinery

- must use planned site entry and exit points only and obey appropriate traffic control procedures
- should use separate routes from pedestrians where practicable; detailed requirements are set out in Section 36 of CDM2007
- should be operated only by trained, authorised and licensed drivers aged 18 years or older
- must comply fully with the Road Traffic Act when it travels on public roads (tax, number plates, lights, brakes etc)
- should have an instruction book detailing the driver's daily checks and routine maintenance
- should have amber rotating lights and reversing siren; in addition a driver should have all-round visibility and mirrors, and CCTV for that purpose shall be positioned carefully, well-maintained in good order at all times
- reversing areas and work sites should be controlled by a banksman and non-essential personnel excluded
- people on site should keep away from a moving or working vehicle/machine until the operator acknowledges he has seen you and stopped activity to let you pass or approach him for conversation
- when tipping into or running alongside excavations must be provided with stop blocks and scotches
- must not be overloaded
- carry only well-secured loads
- must observe site speed limits – these must be clearly signed
- must be immobilised when not in use
- should be parked on level ground, in neutral, with the parking brake applied
- may deposit mud and debris on public roads. Appropriate road cleaning arrangements must be provided
- has limitations on the gradients and cross-slopes on which it can safely operate. These must be observed.

All plant and powered equipment must be operated only by the trained people authorised to use it.

Apart from the risks noted above, there is the risk of damage to hearing and damage to the human body due to vibration. These risks are addressed by the Control of Noise at Work Regulations 2005 (which has guidance L108) and the Control of Vibration at Work Regulations 2005 (which has an ACoP L140 dealing with hand-arm vibration and an ACoP L141 dealing with whole body vibration), which require that limits to exposure to noise and vibration are set out and that cumulative exposure is monitored.

30 Vehicles, machinery and site transport – Bibliography

- HSE (1993) INDG148, *Reversing vehicles*, HSE Books, London (ISBN 0-7176-1063-2)
- HSE (2005) HSG136, *Workplace transport safety: an employer's guide,* 2nd edn, HSE Books, London (ISBN 0-71766-154-7)
- HSE (2005) INDG199Rev1, *Workplace transport safety: an overview*, HSE Books, London (ISBN 0-71762-821-3)
- HSE website: *Vehicles at work* <http://www.hse.gov.uk/workplacetransport/>.

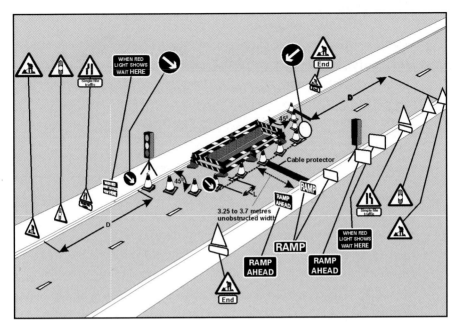

Traffic control on a single carriageway, using portable traffic signals

Note: this sketch indicates the complexity of traffic control signage and equipment. Check with the current version of the manuals referenced below for the latest requirements.

Traffic safety measures at roadworks are covered by the *Traffic signs manual* (1991) and in a simpler form, by *Safety at street works and road works* (2001). Both are available from The Stationery Office.

31 Working on live roads

Planning stage

- local authorities and police must be consulted – and their requirements regarding the timing of the works implemented
- consult *Traffic signs manual* (TSO, 1991) for details of signing requirements and size of safety zones
- decide how many of the following will be required:

  - traffic signs
  - cones
  - barriers

  - road lamps
  - information boards
  - site lighting.

- consider traffic management and control systems
- access must be planned to eliminate dangerous movements of site traffic (eg reversing of vehicles) and personnel (eg crossing dual carriageways)
- will the work be completed in good visibility? If not, adequate lighting must be provided
- all workers must wear high-visibility clothing
- vehicles should be equipped with amber flashing beacons
- minimum lane sizes and provision of adequate safety zones may result in the need for road closures.

On-site

- define the working area in the live road/footway
- define the working space – this includes the areas for storage of tools and equipment and space to move around
- provide a safety zone – an area to separate the work from the traffic – keep it clear of all work, materials storage and people and clear of the working radius of all plant
- work must be undertaken by certificated supervisors and certificated operatives in accordance with the New Roads and Street Works Act.

- Department of Transport (2001) *Safety at Street Works and Road Works A Code of Practice,* TSO, London (ISBN 978-0-11551-958-1)

- Department of Transport (2006) *Traffic signs manual. Chapter 8, Traffic safety measures and signs for road works and temporary situation. Part 1: Design* (2006) (ISBN 978-0-11552-738-8) *Part 2: Operations* (2006) (ISBN 978-0-11552-739-5), TSO, London

- HMSO (1990) *New Roads and Street Works Act 1991,* HMSO, London (ISBN 0-10542-291-6).

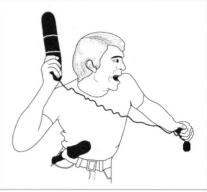

**Combined harness
and life jacket**

Rescue line

Where there is a risk of people falling into water, provision must be made as necessary for:

- risks to be assessed and appropriate activities taken, by avoiding the hazard if possible and reducing risks, so far as is reasonable practicable
- signs to warn of deep water
- edge protection, including guard rails and toe boards
- suitable rescue equipment, and training and instruction in its use
- keeping platforms and ladders clean and clear of debris, slime and tripping hazards
- safety nets to arrest falls where standard working platforms or harnesses cannot be provided
- safety equipment to be maintained properly
- safety lines and harnesses to be used in conjunction with temporary ladder access over water
- site lighting.

The wearing of some types of protective clothing can increase the risk of drowning. Non-slip work boots are preferable to wellington boots; chin straps should not be worn on safety helmets.

Where workers travel on water, the transport shall be safe and not overloaded or overcrowded.

 Boats used for transporting people to/from their place of work must be of suitable construction and size, properly maintained and controlled by competent people.

Rescue equipment

- lifebuoys with rescue lines should be provided at intervals along the site and positioned conveniently for use in an emergency. Floating grab lines should be attached at intervals to structures or floating plant
- personnel must wear lifejackets, or buoyancy aid equipped with a whistle and (during darkness) lights
- before the start of each shift all rescue equipment must be checked by a competent person to ensure it is present and in good condition
- enough personnel should be present who are trained in the use of rescue equipment and emergency procedures.

Rescue boats

- on tidal water or fast-flowing rivers, a power-driven boat should be provided and properly equipped, including lifebuoy with buoyant rope. In certain circumstances, eg some canals and inland waterways, a rowing boat may be sufficient
- where rescue boats are required during the hours of darkness, swivelling searchlights should be fitted
- must be manned continuously during the period that any persons are working over water and when on standby
- must be manned by competent boatmen who are also trained first-aiders
- should not be used for other purposes.

 75 per cent of drownings occur in relatively quiet waters like ponds, reservoirs and rivers.

32 Working over water – Bibliography

- Construction Skills (2008) GE 700 *Construction site safety. Section C3: Working over or near to water* (ISBN 978-1-85751-274-8)

- HSE (2002) HSG177, *Managing health and safety in dock work*, HSE Books, London (ISBN 0-71762-020-4)

- Moth, P (ed) (1998) *Workboat Code of Practice. An operator's guide*, Foreshore Publications Ltd, Hants (ISBN 1-90163-000-5).

Never work alone in the following situations:

- in confined spaces
- over or near water
- on live electrical equipment
- in derelict or dangerous buildings.

If possible, avoid working alone in the following situations:

- on live roads
- in empty buildings
- on roofs
- near demolition work.

Although there is no general legal prohibition on working alone, the hazards that all workers face are increased when there is no one else to give a warning. Also, because there is no one else to help in the event of an accident, the risk of serious injury becomes more likely from:

- tripping, slipping and falling
- becoming trapped or crushed
- electrocution
- asphyxiation.

Plan your work

- risk assessments must be carried out for all lone working where hazards might exist
- evaluate the work to be done – are the workplace and access to it safe? Is more than one person required?
- will any lifting be necessary – can one person do this safely?

Think carefully before you work alone.

33 Working alone

Communicate

- leave details of your movements at a designated place – state where you are going, when you will be there, when you expect to finish and where you will go next
- report in by phone or radio at regular pre-set intervals
- always report in when you leave a site – this is particularly important when you are not returning to your office or normal site base
- if there are other activities in the area make sure your presence is known to those in charge
- take a mobile phone with you whenever possible.

Alarms

Alarms are available that emit a loud emergency siren if the wearer does not move regularly. They are therefore triggered if the wearer is knocked unconscious. They are only effective if someone is within hearing range of the alarm. You should also consider carrying a personal attack alarm.

First aid

- take a small first-aid kit with you
- if you habitually work alone, attend a first-aid course.

Assault

- never admit a stranger into a building if you are working alone
- remember the primary aim is to get away from a dangerous situation
- do not be aggressive – avoid confrontation
- never think that it could not happen to you.

When facing a dangerous situation you MUST act immediately to prevent injury to anyone in the vicinity.

- Suzie Lamplugh Trust. Website guidance sheet G01 *Personal safety at work: a guide for employers and managers* <http://www.suzylamplugh.org/store/ec_products_view.asp?PID=9>

- HSE (2005) INDG73Rev, *Working alone in safety. Controlling the risks of solitary work*, HSE Books, London <http://www.hse.gov.uk/pubns/indg73.pdf>

- Unison (2002) CU12957 *Working alone. A healthy and safety guide on lone working for safety representatives*, Unison, London <http://www.unison.org.uk/acrobat/10943.pdf>.

As soon as you arrive at the site, find out:

- about the site safety organisation and who the site safety supervisors are
- exactly who you report to, and who and what you are responsible for
- how to report hazards that are beyond your control
- where to get further advice
- what personal protective equipment you are required to use, when and where and how to carry out any pre-use checks
- where the first-aid room is and who the first-aiders are
- fire precaution and emergency procedures and services
- bomb warning contingency plans.

Think ahead. Anticipate the safety issues you will face and know the contingency plans, including emergency plans.

Ask to see and read the risk assessments that your employer has prepared for the work.

Read the site notices and act upon them when necessary.

On projects which are "notifiable" find out:

- where the construction phase plan is kept and what it contains
- how you will be made aware of changes in the plan
- how you can contribute to the development of the plan.

If in doubt – find out!

From time to time you will encounter unsafe conditions or unsafe actions. What can you do about them?

Eliminate or reduce hazards, for example, by:

- reporting unsafe practices
- reporting unsafe workplaces
- suggesting alternative means of safer construction
- taking action to stop unsafe activities until the situation has been made safe.

Eliminate or reduce risks, for example by:

- avoiding the risks altogether
- avoiding the activities causing the risks
- wearing appropriate protective clothing and safety equipment
- obeying warning signs and notices
- not putting yourself at risk, even if others are in danger.

On any site or for any site visit, ensure there is a list of contacts and telephone numbers for use in an emergency.

34 Dealing with hazards and risks – Bibliography

- HSE (2007) L144, *Managing health and safety in construction: Construction (Design and Management) legislation 2007. Approved Code of Practice*, HSE Books, London (ISBN 978-0-71766-223-4).

EMERGENCY AID

1 RECOGNISE A LACK OF OXYGEN

Arising from
ELECTRIC SHOCK
DROWNING
POISONING
HEAD INJURY
GASSING etc

May be causing
UNCONSCIOUSNESS

NOISY OR
NO BREATHING

ABNORMAL COLOUR

2 ACT AT ONCE

SWITCH OFF ELECTRICITY, GAS etc
ONLY REMOVE CASUALTY TO PREVENT
FURTHER INJURY
SEND SOMEBODY FOR HELP

GET A CLEAR AIRWAY . . .
REMOVE ANY OBSTRUCTION . . . then

TILT
HEAD BACK

LIFT
JAW

BREATHING MAY RESTART . . . IF NOT . . .

3 APPLY RESCUE BREATHING

START WITH FOUR
QUICK DEEP BREATHS

SEAL NOSE AND
BLOW INTO MOUTH

or

SEAL MOUTH AND
BLOW INTO NOSE

KEEP FINGERS ON JAW
BUT CLEAR OF THROAT

MAINTAIN HEAD
POSITION

AFTER BLOWING INTO
MOUTH or NOSE
WATCH CASUALTY'S
CHEST FALL AS
YOU BREATHE IN

REPEAT EVERY 5 SECS

**AFTER FIRST FOUR
BREATHS TEST FOR
RECOVERY SIGNS**
1. PULSE PRESENT?
2. PUPILS LESS LARGE?
3. COLOUR IMPROVED? **PULSE POINTS**

4 IF NONE, COMBINE RESCUE BREATHING & HEART COMPRESSION

PLACE CASUALTY
ON A FIRM SURFACE

COMMENCE
HEART COMPRESSION

HEEL OF HAND ONLY
ON LOWER HALF OF
BREASTBONE,
OTHER HAND ON TOP
(FINGERS OFF CHEST)

BREASTBONE

HEART

KEEP ARMS STRAIGHT
AND ROCK FORWARD
TO DEPRESS CHEST
40mm

APPLY 15
COMPRESSIONS ONE
PER SECOND . . . then
GIVE TWO BREATHS

RE-CHECK PULSE . . .
IF STILL ABSENT
CONTINUE WITH
15 COMPRESSIONS
TO TWO BREA

IF PULSE RETURNS
CEASE COMPRESSIONS
BUT CONTINUE
RESCUE BREATHING

Rescuers should not put themselves in danger. A second casualty often reduces the chance of providing rapid assistance to the first injured person.

35 Dealing with accidents

Should an accident occur, follow the accident procedures set down by your organisation. These are likely to include:

- send for a first-aider and/or doctor or ambulance
- separate the cause and the victim if possible, eg switch off electricity supplies, turn off powered plant before assisting the casualty
- move a casualty only to prevent further injury
- check the heart and breathing, and give emergency aid as necessary if you have been trained to do so
- stop any bleeding; raise the injured part and apply pressure
- keep the victim warm and reassured
- take care not to become a casualty yourself
- do not remove or disturb evidence

Tell your manager and follow all company incident reporting procedures. Accidents to self-employed people must be reported to the person in control of the workplace. Specific types of accidents must be reported to HSE as soon as possible and always within 10 days (see HSE website for details of when to report under RIDDOR).

Reporting accidents to HSE

Forms for reporting are available through the HSE website or from 01787 881165. You can report by post or telephone, online or by email.

First aid

First-aiders must be readily identifiable – preferably by wearing a distinctive safety helmet. Ensure you know the first-aiders on your site.

You should consider taking a first-aid course. Not only would you learn how to relieve the suffering of an injured colleague, it would help you to stay calm and in control when an accident happens on your site.

Find out whose job it is to report accidents to HSE on your site. It could be yours!

C669 Site safety handbook

- HSE (1997) L74 *First aid at work. The Health and safety (First Aid) Regulations 1981. Approved Code of practice and guidance*, HSE Books, London (ISBN 0-71761-050-0)

- HSE (1999) L73, *A guide to the Reporting of Injuries, Diseases and Dangerous Occurrences Regulations 1995* (RIDDOR), HSE Books, London (ISBN 0-71762-431-5) <http://www.hseni.gov.uk/riddor.pdf>

- HSE (2007) MISC769, *Incident at work?* HSE Books, London <http://www.hse.gov.uk/pubns/misc769.pdf>.

36 Accident investigation

Follow the site procedures of your company and ensure that the competent and named person(s) are informed of the accident or incident. These procedures should include:

- allocating someone to note all the facts immediately and adding these records to the site diary.

If you were a witness or had any responsibility for the work being undertaken when the accident took place you are likely to be required to submit a written report.

Thorough accident investigation has many benefits, including:

- identifying the underlying basic causes
- preventing recurrence of similar accidents
- identifying training needs
- providing information in case of litigation.

Good investigation should highlight the underlying causes and include feedback to designers and managers.

An accident will usually be investigated by:

- the senior site manager
- the company safety adviser
- an HSE inspector may be involved.

You may be asked to help their investigation by providing factual information, so avoid or beware of expressing your personal opinions. Before attending any police, HSE or EHO interview, check with your company directors, risk managers and legal advisors. The nature of the interview must be ascertained and what you and others do will vary depending on what type of interview you are called to. You will also need to know, for example:

- whether someone can or should be present with you
- whether you have to answer any questions
- whether you can stop the interview at any time.

Your organisation should have a policy and procedure to follow to ensure and safeguard your interests and those of your employer. The HSE website offers guidance.

To help you prepare your report, if you witness an accident or are nearby when an accident occurs or if you had any element of managerial control over the work:

- take immediate notes of what you saw and heard
- make sketches of the accident location
- if appropriate, take photographs of the scene and any relevant detail, eg a broken piece of equipment or a missing guard rail. Consider other people's feelings and explain what you are doing
- identify witnesses who actually saw the accident happen – not just those who were present when the accident occurred
- separate fact from hearsay and opinion
- identify, inspect and put aside tools, equipment and materials being used by the injured person(s) at the time of the accident
- check if the work involved a written method statement (other than for rescue) and whether it was being followed
- after your investigation, leave the scene as undisturbed as possible.

Your report will be added to your firm's accident/injury records and provide useful information for future training programmes, accident prevention measures, and for improving company policy and working arrangements.

An investigation by an HSE inspector may lead to criminal proceedings. You may be required to give evidence and your report may be used by the Inspectorate and by your company to help establish the cause of the accident. Remember it is an offence to lie or to cover up the facts.

- HSE (2004) HSG245, *Investigating accidents and incidents, a workbook for employers, unions, safety representatives and safety professionals*, HSE Books, London (ISBN 0-71762-827-2).

- CITB (2008) GE 700, *Construction Site Safety*, CITB
- HMSO (1974) *The Health and Safety at Work etc Act 1974* (ISBN 0-10543-774-3)
- HSE (1996) L24, *Workplace health, safety and welfare. Workplace (Health, Safety and Welfare) Regulations 1992. Approved Code of Practice and guidance*, HSE Books, London (ISBN 0-71760-413-6) <http://www.hse.gov.uk/pubns/indg244.pdf>
- HSE (1997) HSG65, *Successful health and safety management*, HSE Books, London (ISBN 0-71761-276-7)
- HSE (1999) SI 1999/3242, *The Management of Health and Safety at Work Regulations 1999*, HSE Books, London (ISBN 0-11085-625-2)
- HSE (2006) HSG150, *Health and safety in construction*, 3rd edn, HSE Books, London (ISBN 0-71766-182-2).

HSE publications and public information points

Information

For health and safety information and advice, contact the HSE public enquiry point:

HSE Infoline

0845 450055

email: hse.infoline@natbrit.com

website: <http://www.hse.gov.uk/contact/ask.htm>

Publications

All HSE publications are available from:

HSE Books

PO Box 1999

Sudbury

Suffolk CO10 6FS

Tel: 01787 881165

website: <http://www.hsebooks.com/books>

All HSE current publications are listed in *Publication in series* which is updated regularly and is available through the Internet.